Educating for Values-Driven Leadership

Educating for Values-Driven Leadership

Giving Voice to Values Across the Curriculum

Mary C. Gentile, PhD

First published in 2013 by
Business Expert Press, LLC
222 East 46th Street, New York, NY 10017
www.businessexpertpress.com

ISBN-13: 978-1-60649-546-9 (paperback)
ISBN-13: 978-1-60649-547-6 (e-book)

Business Expert Press Principles of Responsible Management Education
(PRME) Collection

Collection ISSN: Forthcoming (print)
Collection ISSN: Forthcoming (electronic)

Cover and interior design by Exeter Premedia Services Private Ltd.
Chennai, India

First edition: 2013

10 9 8 7 6 5 4 3 2 1

Printed in the United States of America.

Abstract

Despite four decades of good faith effort to teach Ethics in business schools, readers of the business press are still greeted on a regular basis with headlines about egregious excess and scandal. It becomes reasonable to ask why these efforts have not been working.

Business faculty in ethics courses spend a lot of time teaching theories of ethical reasoning and analyzing those big, thorny dilemmas—triggering what one professor called "ethics fatigue." Some students find such approaches intellectually engaging; others find them tedious and irrelevant. Either way, sometimes all they learn is how to frame the case to justify virtually any position, no matter how cynical or self-serving. Utilitarianism, after all, is tailor-made for a free market economy.

As for those "ethical dilemmas," too often they are couched as choices that only a chief executive could love—because only a CEO would confront them. The average 30-year-old MBA graduate is not likely to decide whether to run that pipeline across the pristine wilderness or whether to close the company's manufacturing plant.

It's not that ethical theory and high-level strategic dilemmas are not important; unquestionably they are. But they don't help future managers and leaders figure out what to do the next—when a boss wants to alter the financial report, or their sales team applies pressure to misrepresent the capabilities of their product, or they witness discrimination against a peer—and *these* are the experiences that will shape their ability to take on the strategic, thorny ethical dilemmas in time.

The near-term skill set revolves around **what to say, to whom, and how to say it** when the manager knows what he or she *thinks is right* when an ethical breech occurs—but doesn't feel confident about how to *act* on his or her convictions. This overlooked but consequential skill set is the first step in building the ethical muscle. This is the purpose of the *Giving Voice to Values* program.

Faculty at business schools from MIT to INSEAD to Notre Dame to Columbia Busines School to the University of Queensland to the Goa Institute of Management, among many others, have used or developed elements of the pilot curriculum. Our goal is to both build a conversation across the core curriculum (not only in ethics courses) and to also provide the teaching aids and curriculum for a new way of thinking about ethics education. Rather than a focus on ethical *analysis*, the *Giving Voice to Values* (*GVV*) curriculum focuses on ethical *implementation* and asks the question: "What if I were going to act on my values? What would I say and do? How could I be most effective?"

In *Educating for Values-Driven Leadership: Giving Voice to Values Across the Curriculum*, faculty across the business curriculum will find examples, strategies, and assistance in applying the GVV approach in their required and elective courses. In addition to an introductory chapter which explains the rationale and strategy behind GVV, there are twelve individual chapters by faculty from the major business functional areas and from faculty representing different geographic regions. The book is a useful guide for faculty from any business discipline on HOW to use the GVV approach in his or her teaching, and it can also serve as a brief background reading for students who are embarking on their business studies, encouraging them to take the GVV approach to their studies, whether or not it is explicitly introduced in every course.

Keywords

business ethics, management education, business education, pedagogy, values, values-driven leadership, cross-functional education, environmental and social impacts management, corporate social responsibility, sustainability, CSR communication, stakeholder communication.

Contents

PART 1

Introduction to Giving Voice to Values

CHAPTER 1

Educating for Values-Driven Leadership

Giving Voice to Values Across the Curriculum

Mary C. Gentile

Abstract

Traditional approaches to education for values-driven leadership in management education have lacked an emphasis on actual rehearsal—the preparation for action that builds confidence as well as competence. Giving Voice to Values is an innovative pedagogy and curriculum that addresses this gap. Its focus is on literal prescripting and action planning, and it was developed to directly address the challenges faced by educators in the core business functions when they consider ways to integrate discussions of values into their curriculum. Its rapid adoption, across business functions and around the world and in businesses as well as educational settings, demonstrates its usefulness.

Keywords

leadership, values, ethics, business ethics, *Giving Voice to Values*, pedagogy, curriculum, management education, business education.

Author Biography

Mary C. Gentile, PhD, is director of *Giving Voice to Values* [www .GivingVoicetoValues.org], launched with The Aspen Institute and Yale

School of Management, now based at and funded by Babson College. This pioneering curriculum for values-driven leadership has hundreds of pilot sites globally and has been featured in *Financial Times, Harvard Business Review, Stanford Social Innovation Review, McKinsey Quarterly,* etc. Gentile, Senior Research Scholar at Babson College and educational consultant, was previously faculty and administrator at Harvard Business School for 10 years. She holds a BA from The College of William and Mary and PhD from State University of New York-Buffalo. Gentile's publications include: *Giving Voice to Values: How to Speak Your Mind When You Know What's Right* (Yale University Press, Summer 2010, www. MaryGentile.com); Can *Ethics Be Taught? Perspectives, Challenges, and Approaches at Harvard Business School* (with Thomas Piper & Sharon Parks); *Differences That Work: Organizational Excellence through Diversity; Managerial Excellence Through Diversity: Text and Cases,* as well as cases and articles in *Academy of Management Learning and Education, Harvard Business Review, Risk Management, CFO, BizEd, Strategy+Business,* etc. Gentile was content expert for the award-winning CD-ROM, *Managing Across Differences.*

Origins and Rationale Behind the *Giving Voice to Values* Approach

Increasingly "Values-Driven Leadership"—the aspiration, the competency and the commitment—has become an explicit objective for business educators and business practitioners alike. The prevailing wisdom is that organizations that want to insure ethical decision making and behavior in the workplace will do better by appealing to employee values and by affirming positive organizational goals, than by focusing exclusively or even primarily on a rules and compliance orientation. Business and educational thoughts leaders from Jim Collins to Lynn Sharp Paine have made this point, and the emphasis on leadership curriculum in management education is a reflection of this shift.

Ethics education in business schools, however, although also receiving an increasing amount of attention—often not so positive—from the management education accrediting bodies, from the business press and, accordingly, from business school deans, has not always reflected the power of this aspiration and competency-based orientation. In fact, business ethics education has too often remained the realm of "thou shalt not" rather than appealing to a sense of purpose and building a skill-based confidence and moral competence. For business students and practitioners, ethics education's emphasis on action constraints is not very appealing. These are the sorts of people who are motivated by the desire for achievement and accomplishment; they want to build enterprises, to create new products and services, to reach new markets and, of course, to make money. Accordingly, to make education for ethics and values compelling and useful for this audience, it becomes important to link it to action—effective, impactful action. Instead of focusing on what we cannot do, it becomes important to ask and answer the questions: How can we act on our values? How can we build our business based on values? How can we be effective as well as ethical?

Giving Voice to Values[1] (GVV)—an innovative pedagogy and curriculum, launched by the Aspen Institute Business and Society Program as incubator and, along with Yale School of Management, founding partner, and now based and supported at Babson College—is crafted as a response to just these questions. GVV identifies the many ways that individuals can and do voice their values in the workplace and provides opportunities to build the muscles necessary to do so.

GVV grew out of two recognitions: first, that increasingly research from a variety of different disciplines—social psychology, cognitive neurosciences, even kinesthetics—suggested that an effective way to influence behavioral choices was through rehearsal—literal practice; and second, that traditional approaches to ethics and values education tended to focus on building Awareness and teaching Analysis—both cognitive skills—to the exclusion of this same "rehearsal" and its focus on Action. It is not that Awareness (so we can recognize ethical challenges we encounter them) and Analysis (so we can discipline our reasoning about those same challenges, in order to identify the right course of Action) are not important and necessary; they unquestionably are essential. It is rather that they are not sufficient, and in many ways, the emphasis on Action as outlined in the GVV pedagogy is a better fit with the other, nonethics courses across the business curriculum.

These core recognitions formed the basis for the GVV pedagogy. A new type of case exercise was developed with several distinguishing features. The cases are typically brief and therefore easy for faculty across the curriculum to fit them into their syllabi and to assign them as group exercises for students. They feature managers at all levels of the organization, from new managers just out of school, to mid-level managers, all the way through to senior and C-suite executives; in this way, the cases are adaptable for undergraduate, graduate, and executive education purposes, reflecting the fact that students will be encountering and responding to values conflicts right from the start. The cases are based on real situations, although almost always disguised, and as often as possible feature examples of occasions when the case protagonist was, in fact, able to positively resolve the challenge presented. Most importantly and distinctively, however, these GVV cases conclude at a point where their protagonist has already decided what he or she believes the "right" thing to do is and the question becomes: How can they get it done effectively? In this way, the students' work individually and in teams to investigate, research, craft, and present the best and most feasible literal script and action plan for enacting the protagonist's values-based position.

When the students share their best solutions to the case challenge, their classmates are invited to engage in a peer-coaching dialogue where the focus is not on a simple critique of their colleagues' "solutions" but rather on collaborating to enhance and improve them. In this way, the students are invited into what is called the "GVV Thought Experiment." Rather than being presented with an ethical challenge and asked "what would you do?"—a question that can invite "easy" or naïve posturing or skeptical resistance—instead they are presented with a values-driven position and asked how they might successfully enact it. In this way, when they do actually face this decision, they can see that they actually have a choice; they have strategies, tactics, exemplars, and scripts for approaching it. They still do, in fact, have to make that choice, but the GVV curriculum has prepared them to have actual options. There are no easy assurances, but rather a recognition that we are all more likely to do things that we have seen work before or that we have practiced ourselves, preferably in tandem with our peers. The students are not asked to commit to something that they do not, in their heart of hearts, think is possible. Instead, they are enabled to build approaches they can believe in.

Other features of the curriculum that prepare students to engage in these scripting, action planning, and peer coaching exercises include an emphasis on self-assessment so that they can "play to their strengths" when it comes to selecting an effective communication style or problem framing; an introduction to research on cognitive biases and decision-making biases and how they might be used to reframe choices and craft effective arguments; and the opportunity to identify and practice responses to some of the most frequently heard arguments for NOT acting on one's values (the "reasons and rationalizations" in GVV parlance). All of these features are explained and illustrated in detail in the curricular materials.[2]

How Giving Voice to Values Is Used in Business Education

Now, of course, to make this educational shift, faculty members hold the key. And while the GVV curriculum and pedagogy were created as a response to the insight that education for action is a critical part of values-driven leadership development, it was also designed with an eye to the specific concerns that faculty often hold when it comes to business ethics education.

The integration of values and ethics education across the business curriculum has long been a "holy grail" for those who endeavor to promote this sort of leadership development. This is not to say that stand-alone ethics courses are not important and necessary, both as opportunities to dive deep into the insights of those who specialize in this arena and as opportunities to serve as curriculum-development engines to create and pilot test new materials that can work their way out into the other disciplines; they are. It is simply to say that the answer to the ages-old debate around "integration of ethics versus stand-alone" courses is "Yes and Yes." That is, without also integrating these issues into the other courses, they are often marginalized at best, or even discredited at worst in the rest of the core curriculum.

However, although we have yet to meet a professor of finance or accounting or operations management who did not want his or her students to become responsible and ethical managers, these same faculty members often have several strong objections to the integration of explicit discussions of ethics and values into their courses. They do not want to raise issues for which they feel they are unprepared (e.g., "I am trained as an economist, not an ethicist."). They don't want to appear to be preaching to their students and they don't want to seem naïve. They don't want to be in the uncomfortable position of advocating a position that they are not sure is feasible; after all, these educators know that their students are likely to encounter very real and strong pressures to violate their own ethics at some points in their careers. Additionally, their syllabi are already very full with the skills and concepts that are central to their respective disciplines—accounting, marketing, etc.—and it is hard to justify inserting time for discussions that very often lead to no specific conclusion or "take-aways," as far as the professors and students can see.

These reasonable and legitimate faculty concerns have been key drivers in the design of the GVV curriculum. First of all, the curriculum is "post-decision-making," as Carolyn Woo, former business school dean at University of Notre Dame, observed. That is, the cases feature protagonists who have already identified what they believe the right thing to do would be, and the questions become: How can they get it done, effectively and efficiently? What do they need to say, to whom, and in what sequence? What will the objections or push-back be and, then, what would they say next? What data and examples do they need? And so on. In this way, faculty do not need to be in the position to be arguing with students about whether they should or whether they can act on their values in the workplace. Instead, the focus shifts to the question of "how" they could do so successfully.

Similarly, GVV builds on the expertise and the teaching objectives of the business discipline-based faculty because students are not using the language and the tools of philosophy to create their scripts and action-plans, but rather the language and the analytical frameworks of the functional area that is relevant to the issue at hand and the course where it is raised. So if the course is Managerial Accounting and the case is about a CFO pressured to "cook the books"[3] the scripts and action plans will be about calculating and communicating the internal and external costs of this practice (not only the cost of detection, but also the cost of distorted information inside the firm, for example).

Thus, the very foundation of the GVV pedagogy and curriculum— that is, an emphasis on asking "how to act ethically?" rather than why or even if one can do so—by definition and design, serves as a sort of pedagogical sleight of hand, enabling the faculty across the business core to includes values-driven leadership issues in their syllabi more comfortably, more effectively, and even more appropriately than in the past.

Additionally, GVV curriculum is designed flexibly so that it can be adopted easily by the individual faculty member in an accounting or a marketing course who wants to find a way to do so, or, alternatively, it can be orchestrated across the entire curriculum at those schools where faculty and deans have decided to take a more systematic approach to the integration of values and ethics. In the former case, the individual faculty member can simply access the hundreds of pages of short cases and readings and exercises, all available for free download at www.GivingVoiceToValues .org. The "Annotated Table of Contents" for the curriculum identifies the materials that can work in each of the various business courses, whether that may be economics or organizational behavior. And there is another website, available on request to faculty only, which includes teaching notes and "B" cases as well.

If, however, a school's faculty and deans wish to use GVV more systematically in order to integrate values across the entire curriculum, it is helpful to sequence the building blocks of this approach—foundational exercises ("A Tale of Two Stories"; "Starting Assumptions for GVV" "Personal–Professional Profiles"); the scripting and action-planning tools, and the scenario-based rehearsals in different functional classes—across the core courses.

Finally, some faculty have piloted a dedicated elective or core course that introduces students to the GVV pedagogy and even engages them in generating their own GVV-style cases and case solutions. An essay describing all of these approaches ("How Business Schools and Faculty Can Use the Giving Voice to Values Curriculum") is available on the curriculum website and individualized guidance is available from the program director.

The Purpose of This Book

GVV was developed with the twin objectives of creating an effective approach to building the capacity for values-driven action in business students and practitioners and also of structuring the curriculum in a way that would be useful and appealing to faculty across the curriculum. This book is intended as an opportunity to explicitly further the second of these goals. Individual faculty members from across the business curriculum have been invited to write chapters describing how they have begun to pilot and adapt the GVV pedagogy in their own teaching. The hope is that the professor of economics or of accounting or of public administration or of marketing and so on will not only find ideas and encouragement in the chapter written by one of his or her peers, but also will be intrigued enough to read and learn from the other chapters where faculty across the disciplines share their experiences and their learnings with this new pedagogy.

Readers will find that some of the GVV exercises and cases can work well in multiple disciplines (e.g., "'This Whole System Seems Wrong': Felipe Montez and Concerns about the Global Supply Chain"), while others are more tailored for a particular function. They will also see that much of GVV is counter to our habitual assumptions about how to think about and teach ethics. This is both a reason for the efficacy and appeal of the approach, and an occasional challenge.

For example, some faculty members have encountered initial cynicism when introducing the GVV materials, particularly when working with practitioners. However, in our experience, this cynicism often abates once the concept of the "GVV Thought Experiment" is presented, explaining that no one is being asked to commit to a particular course of action but rather to work, hard and rigorously and collectively, to develop a plan that they could, in fact, find feasible. The cynicism is often born from the assumption that no one else cares about these values or that they are just not possible. The sharing of positive examples of individuals who have, in fact, found ways to enact their ethics, and providing opportunities for students, with their peers, to "try on" the idea that this sort of action is possible, can enable them to begin to pursue their values without feeling naïve or vulnerable.

Another way that traditional approaches to ethics education can be confounded by GVV is in relation to the use of role-playing. Often when role playing is used in an ethics discussion, it is set up as an adversarial exchange: one student plays the role of the person who is concerned about the infraction and another plays the manager who is pressuring their report to oversell the product's capabilities, or to distort the quarterly earnings statement, for example. The problem with this sort of adversarial role-play is that we are all more easily able to generate the arguments for the unethical choice. We have grown up with these "reasons and rationalizations" and it can be kind of fun to "play the villain." To effectively counter these arguments, and to not feel naïve while doing so, students need to spend the time that the GVV scripting and action planning requires of them. They need to work together to research and refine their approaches; to figure out what is at stake for all involved; where the "levers" of influence may lie; how they might reframe the choice so as to neutralize the objections; and even what sort of approach (individual or collective, private or public, oral or written, quantitative or qualitative) will be most effective with one's particular target audience. For all these reasons, the GVV scripting, action planning, and peer coaching exercise is NOT the typical adversarial role-play. Rather, all the students are "on the same side," working together to try to come up with the most effective and feasible approach. This is not to say that traditional role-plays cannot be useful in some contexts, but they run the risk of asking students to "rehearse" the very behaviors we are trying to discourage. And most importantly, it is helpful to recognize that ethics education is developmental and it is important to build the "moral muscle memory" via rehearsal and peer coaching before moving to the adversarial exchange.

Finally, one more way that GVV runs counter to traditional approaches to ethics education centers on the types of decisions the curriculum features. Often educators and students and practitioners alike will argue that the so-called easy or clear-cut ethical conflicts are not a problem, but that it is the "gray" issue, the time when things are neither clearly right nor clearly wrong, that is truly difficult. And, therefore, they argue, ethics education should ignore the easy questions and focus on these ambiguous decisions.

With GVV, we take a different stance. We acknowledge that, of course, there are many of these thorny ethical choices where the right path is not evident; these are the true ethical "dilemmas" and they are important. But we argue that these "gray" issues are actually often instances where reasonable people of good will and intelligence can legitimately disagree: that's why they are "gray"! And, in contrast, just because an issue is clear-cut, it does not mean that it is easy to act on it. In fact, many of the ethical violations that have led to growing distrust of the business sector were occasions when the action in question was indeed clearly over the line, in the realm of illegality and fraud. And, in many of those instances, we learn of employees who were, in fact, aware of what was going on and were not happy about it, but who did not feel they had any options. So GVV focuses on those issues—the so-called clear cut issues—and asks how could we act on our values in those situations? Rather than getting lost in an endless and answer-less debate over the gray issues, GVV provides the opportunity to focus on actual arguments and tactics for the times when the "right" choice is perhaps more evident but no less challenging to enact.

Giving Voice to Values has spread rapidly across the globe, with hundreds of pilots reaching thousands of students and business practitioners on all seven continents. Increasingly major corporations are applying this approach to their own internal ethics, values, and leadership programming as well. None of this would have been possible without the commitment and willingness of individual faculty, such as the authors featured in this volume, to engage in this experiment. In fact, these faculty—especially these authors—are the ambassadors of an emerging movement. Together they are part of an effort that holds the promise to transform the foundational assumptions on which the teaching of business ethics is based, and importantly, to equip future business leaders to not only know what is right—but also how to make it happen.

PART 2

GVV Across
the Curriculum

CHAPTER 2

Giving Voice to Values in the Economics Classroom

Daniel G. Arce

Abstract

This chapter demonstrates the use of Giving Voice to Values (GVV) within the context of real-world issues commonly found in the economics curriculum. It begins with a motivating example to raise ethical awareness when dealing with issues as basic as supply and demand. The use of GVV is then expanded upon through an illustrative case centered on the comparative statics of market equilibrium subsequent to a natural disaster, as applied to Waffle House's postdisaster menu/pricing policies. The chapter concludes with a discussion on how to facilitate the use of GVV with economics students who may be initially circumspect about the integration of ethics within an economics course.

Keywords

Giving Voice to Values, economics, supply and demand, natural disasters, Waffle House.

Author Biography

Daniel G. Arce M., is professor of Economics at the University of Texas—Dallas, where he is also the Program Head. He holds a PhD in Economics from the University of Illinois at Urbana-Champaign and has published over 50 articles on business ethics, collective action, game theory, (counter)terrorism, and Latin American economies. He has received two Fulbright grants for study and research in Latin

America. Professor Arce is the editor of *Defence and Peace Economics*, serves on the editorial board of *The Southern Economic Journal* and the reviewing team for the teaching business ethics section of *Journal of Business Ethics*. His teaching has been profiled in *The Wall Street Journal* and his research in *The Economist*.

Introduction and Background

The topic (of what money should and should not be allowed to buy) falls a bit between the cracks of business school professors, who often hate to raise ethical problems, and economists, who don't always know what ethical problems are.

—Stanley Hoffman (in Standel (2005))

When I introduce Giving Voice to Values (hereafter, GVV) I like to begin with the following set of questions, which I have asked students in principles of economics; upper level undergraduate classes on managerial economics; and executives in MBA modules on business economics.

1. In the market for candles what is the expected effect on the equilibrium price and quantity if there is a decrease in supply and an increase in demand?
2. If the price of paraffin (used to make candles) rises and, at the same time, a candle fad breaks out, what is the expected effect on the equilibrium price and quantity of candles?
3. If a natural disaster (hurricane, tornado, volcanic eruption, flood, earthquake, etc.) occurs that knocks out all power and disrupts the local supply chain for candles, what is the expected effect on the equilibrium price and quantity of candles?

As supply and demand is the entrée into almost any course on (micro) economics, it is easy to fit in this set of questions, and thus an introduction to GVV, early on in the semester. Two points that illustrate the utility of GVV within economics that stem from these questions are as follows. First, from the perspective of the comparative statics of supply and demand, the above questions are equivalent. A decrease in supply and an increase in demand produce an expected increase in the price of candles, with the impact on quantity depending on the relative magnitudes of the decrease in supply and increase in demand. Any price below the market-clearing price will create a shortage. Perhaps one can make the case that supply is temporarily (perfectly) price inelastic while demand has substantially increased (e.g., the time period is Marshallian[1]); but price will be expected to increase in any event. Second, in practice the prices of necessary goods usually do not increase in the aftermath of a natural disaster. Indeed, prices often fall even in the face of restricted supply after disasters. This was first shown to be the case for necessary food-stuffs in grocery stores during the recovery after the Alaskan Good Friday earthquake of 1964 (Kunreuther and Fiore, 1966; Kunreuther, 1967), and remains a contemporary phenomenon, as evidenced by regional gasoline prices in Texas after Hurricane Rita in 2005 (Neilson, 2009). Hence, when one hears about "price gouging" in the aftermath of natural disasters, it is newsworthy because it is so contrary to the norm.[2]

This simple set of questions capitalizes on what I have consistently observed as the inability of economics majors to recognize that the ethical context of question 3 above is not the same as that for questions 1 and 2. Indeed, just as the epigraph to this chapter indicates, the loss of ethical awareness in conjunction with education in economics is becoming well documented. Such concerns have been previously raised by Frank (2004) within the context of the prevalence of "noncooperators" among economists in Prisoner's Dilemma experiments as compared to other majors; and by Rubinstein (2006), in which economics majors and PhD students see the profit-maximizing amount of layoffs during a recession as primarily a technical issue, whereas those with alternative educational backgrounds see the issue of layoffs from a more nuanced perspective.[3] Indeed, over the past decade, my classroom discussion of question 3 with hundreds of economics majors within a liberal arts environment has made it clear that the vast majority of majors initially approach question 3 as being equivalent to questions 1 and 2 until the ethical context is explicitly pointed out. This is entirely consistent with the widespread absence of an ethical perspective in managerial economics textbooks (Arce, 2004).

Marwell and Ames (1981), Miller (1999), Ferraro et al. (2005), and Molinsky et al. (2012) assert that what the issue is really about is why self-interest takes precedence for economists, but not others, when establishing a pecking order of criteria for evaluating scenarios such as the Prisoner's Dilemma, the Ultimatum Game, choosing layoffs during a recession, raising prices during a natural disaster, invoking one's own compassion when delivering bad news to others, etc. If training in how to make self-interested decisions explains differences between the economically trained and others in these and other packaged scenarios and this extends to meaningful differences in the real world then there may because for concern. Within the context of the three questions that opened this chapter, reputable firms generally do not raise prices in the immediate aftermath of a natural disaster because much more is at stake than the prospect of short-term profits. Indeed, Waffle House, Wal-Mart, Lowes, and Home Depot all generate significant goodwill because of the firms' postdisaster solidarity with their local communities (Ergun et al., 2010; Bauerlein, 2011).

Some broad guidelines for introducing (business) ethics into economics and financial economics classrooms are provided by Aragon (2011), Arce (2004, 2011), Eriksson (2005), Northrup (2000), and Welch (2006). Popular statements exist that are anathema to these attempts, such as Levitt and Dubner's (2005, p. 13) assertion in *Freakonomics* that, "morality, it could be argued, represents the way that people would like the work to work—whereas economics represents the way it actually *does* work" (emphasis in original). Does this mean that the tools of comparative statistics are what is best put to bear in addressing pricing after a natural disaster? As the evidence suggests that the movement in prices in natural disasters is contrary to what would be indicated by economic analysis, I argue that what is needed is the placement of ethical analysis on the same footing and in the same context as economic analysis. To address concerns about economic education and ethical (un)awareness, students could also be given opportunities to see and discuss scenarios such as question 3 so that the stakes between economic and ethical perspectives are normalized. Making ethical arguments requires the same sort of practice that makes a student conversant in the tools of economic analysis.

This is where *Giving Voice to Values* (Gentile, 2010) comes in. GVV is a freely available curriculum of cases and scripts that allow students to articulate ethical arguments in familiar economics and business situations.

Hence, as GVV falls naturally within the curriculum, it economizes on the scarcity of classroom time. I have found that the GVV case considered in this chapter—and others on cases appropriate to an economics classroom on topics such as profit maximization and layoffs, product recall, etc.—take up about 30 minutes of classroom time. My usual practice is to cover one case during class so that students get the gist of the approach and assign three to four cases throughout the semester as group projects.

In other words, GVV does not require stepping outside of the normal functioning of the classroom for an "ethics break" unrelated to the course material. Indeed, it purposefully does not require that nonethics faculty educate students in the constructs of normative decision making, although it acknowledges and is complementary to the foundation provided in dedicated ethics courses. Bazerman and Tenbrunsel (2011, p. 155) contend that GVV can help to create awareness of the ethical dimensions of a situation because the GVV rubric forces those adopting it to identify the major issues involved in a decision in a systematic and comprehensive way. For example, in this chapter, I present a case involving a real-world scenario for pricing in the aftermath of a natural disaster without reference to formal normative ethical theory. In so doing I illustrate the general applicability of GVV to economic decision making by examining the potential ethical component of a common business issue (whether or not to raise prices).

This chapter illustrates the utility of including GVV cases within the economics curriculum and provides a guideline for doing so. I begin with a GVV case pertaining to Waffle House Restaurant's pricing policy subsequent to natural disasters that builds off the motivating questions in the introduction. In addition to providing brief details pertaining to the protagonist's resolution of the scenario, I provide talking points for the three areas of discussion normally addressed in a GVV case: (a) what is at stake for the key parties, (b) what arguments or rationalizations are the protagonists tying to counter, and (c) what levers can the protagonist use in order to influence those with whom s/he disagrees. This is done in order to better facilitate a discussion of these open-ended questions. In an actual GVV classroom exercise (or group assignment), students are required to generate these arguments and decision reframings themselves.

The Waffle House Case

In class I begin my introduction to GVV with the supply and demand questions that opened this chapter. As the vast majority of students (no matter whether they are undergraduates or executive MBAs) initially see the three questions as being equivalent, students become somewhat chagrined when I point out that a decision to raise prices during a natural disaster has ethical implications that they may have overlooked. I then briefly discuss some background literature on the relation between an education focused on concepts such as self-interest, rationality, and efficiency and what this does to ethical awareness. Examples of such studies include Frank (2004), Rubinstein (2006), Arce and Li (2011), and Molisnky et al. (2012). As a whole, this process provides sufficient prompting for students to be open to considering the ethical dimension to what they might otherwise see as a purely economic problem. I then turn to the following case.

Reggie Smith is the manager of a Waffle House Restaurant in a region that has recently experienced a local disaster (hurricane, tornado, volcanic eruption, flood, earthquake, etc.). Power is out almost everywhere but he can keep his restaurant open, due to the emergency generator the restaurant always has on-hand to keep the lights on and the ability to switch fuels used to power the grill by means of a several-day supply of gas in tanks.

The grill is the only thing that can be used to cook with at the moment. This means a limited menu, constructed by keeping in mind what is easiest to prepare and what people want most. The limited menu decision has far-reaching implications; as FEMA in fact has a "Waffle House Index" to measure the severity of a disaster. According to the index, Green corresponds to a full menu; Yellow means a limited menu (power from a generator and low food supplies); and Red corresponds to a closed restaurant. Reggie knows FEMA will be calling soon. The information he provides will be consistent with Yellow.

The available items and their normal menu prices are given in Table 2.1.[4]

Table 2.1. The Limited Menu

Menu item	Normal price	Menu item	Normal price
Waffle	$2.80	Hash Browns	$1.50
Pecan Waffle	$3.25	Large Hash Browns	$2.05
Two Eggs, Toast, & Grits/Hash Browns	$3.15	Grits	$1.50
Sausage & Egg Sandwich	$3.15	Sausage	$2.30
Sausage & Egg Biscuit	$1.40	City Ham	$2.50
Ham & Egg Sandwich	$3.15	Cereal with Milk	$1.85
Ham & Egg Biscuit	$1.40	Pastries	$1.90
Sausage Biscuit	$1.05	Pie	$2.00
¼ lb. Hamburger	$2.70	Coffee	$1.35
Double ¼ lb. Hamburger	$3.45	Alice's Iced Tea	$1.45
Chicken Sandwich	$3.15	Milk	$1.45
Grilled Ham & Cheese Sandwich	$3.55	Large Milk	$1.65
Grilled Cheese Sandwich	$2.00	Soft Drinks	$1.45
¼ lb. Hamburger, Hash Browns + Drink	$5.70	OJ (Large)	$1.00
Chicken Sandwich, Hash Browns + Drink	$6.20	Service Charge on "To Go" items	10%

Reggie anticipates volume of more than 2–3 times of what is normal. Moreover, because of the limited menu he is going to have to write the available items and their prices on a blackboard, which means that he can change the prices if he desires. He also has the latitude to change prices; particularly if costs have dramatically changed. He currently has food on hand and Waffle House has a policy of restocking from surrounding restaurants that are outside the disaster area. He does not expect prolonged supply disruptions because his primary supplier also provides food to hospitals (this choice of supplier is by design). At the same time, it is more costly to keep the lights on with a generator and run the grill out of gas tanks. Although it is not mandatory, it is recommended to check with HQ if considering a price change.

Reggie is resolute that the prices should not change and should retain their predisaster values. With this in mind, I ask students to form groups of three to five members and answer the following discussion questions in terms of the broader context of not raising prices on necessary goods in the immediate aftermath of a natural disaster. They should write down at least three answers to each question.

Discussion Questions

In this section I present the questions corresponding to the GVV rubric, along with talking points in order to better stimulate conversation. In an actual GVV exercise, students are asked to provide these responses but I have found that it is helpful to have some answers on hand to further stimulate discussion, particularly for faculty and students who are new to GVV.

What is at stake for the key parties, including those with whom Reggie disagrees?
It is often helpful to identify all stakeholders in order to fully understand the ethical dimensions of a decision. Stakeholders include customers who need food and could use a return to any degree of normalcy that the Waffle House experience can provide. Identifying with customers allows one to realize that people are more vulnerable when participating in markets than they usually are. Consumers can no longer exit from exchange with reasonable expectations of finding better terms elsewhere or by delaying purchases.

In addition, Waffle House itself has several interested parties. Reggie may be putting his job at stake if HQ does not agree with his pricing decision. It is also likely that he lives in the community so his personal reputation is on the line. Waffle House's local employees could use the paycheck to help finance their disaster recovery. At the same time, these employees may have other disaster-related demands on their time that imply that Waffle House may have a labor supply issue. As for the local franchise, it has to face a public relations issue regarding any pricing decision. Reggie's decision to keep prices as they are is consistent with communicating an ethos of integrity and empathy toward those enduring hardship. Yet the local franchise is going to have to absorb higher costs and the disaster does not remove its need to make a profit. Finally, Waffle House's HQ does not want to be found in violation of price gauging laws (which most states have; one of the benefits of the GVV approach is that it provides an opportunity to share such information); or worse—it does not want to damage the brand's image, either through its pricing or providing a diminished experience owing to the degraded operating environment. Like any firm, Waffle House's reputation can be expressed as a function of the difference between its customer's expectations and their actual experience. Both price increases and service quality must be taken into account when considering the expectation/experience reputational trade-off.

Disparate interests are also held by other parties. For example, FEMA needs an accurate report of the circumstances so that it can adequately react to the crisis. FEMA actually does have a Waffle House Index that helps to guide the level of assistance that the community will receive. Waffle House's suppliers also have to make their own pricing decisions and may react to price increases by Waffle House with increases of their own. Regulators will be on the lookout for evidence of price gouging. This is a situation that may merit regulation as asymmetric information exists because sellers have better information about post disaster supplies than do customers. In addition, Waffle House's competitive environment has changed in that it has more monopoly power.

What are the main arguments that Reggie is trying to counter? That is, what are the reasons and rationalizations that he needs to address?
This case is tailor-made for the economics classroom because many of the arguments here are familiar to students. For example, arguments to raise prices often echo economic arguments that criticize price gouging laws. Specifically, at a price below the equilibrium level a shortage will occur. Prices should adjust to reflect the potential for shortages and encourage a market-based resolution of shortages. Not changing prices would prevent the remedy of shortages through the price-as-rationing mechanism. Even if those who are most willing to pay are income-constrained and cannot buy the good at the higher prices, the higher prices still encourage both conservation and out-of-region sellers to bring necessary goods to the affected region. It may be preferred to encourage increased supply

by local and national firms through increased prices, because these will be tempered owing to a concern for reputation, rather than consumers having to resolve shortages and risk fraud by dealing with out-of-region fly-by-night sellers who have no reputation whatsoever and may never be seen again.

There are also perspectives that are internal to the firm. For example, costs and workloads are higher so it is reasonable to increase prices. The firm is raising prices to cover costs, not to increase profits. In particular, Reggie's decision to remain open should be subject to the familiar shut-down decision: Given that his average variable costs have increased, prices should cover average variable costs in order to remain open. From a longer term perspective, one must be concerned that any short-term losses do not damage the long-term viability of the local restaurant. From an antiregulatory viewpoint, in the absence of shortages the firm is able to charge what consumers are willing to pay, so why should the case of a disaster be any different? Moreover, Waffle House is not responsible for the natural disaster/disruptive event; hence, it is not like it is exploiting something that is under its control.

Noneconomic arguments can also be made on behalf of a price increase. Students often come up with a perspective that is consistent with the *principle of proportionality*: One must balance the potential harm done to the firm of not increasing prices with the harms caused by raising prices. From this perspective, the community will expect and understand a "reasonable" price increase. Yet, according to the entitlement theory (Kahneman et al., 1986), it is more accepted by consumers to raise prices when the price increase is tied to the costs associated with a particular good or service than if the increased costs are associated with doing business in general. This is particularly true with disaster-related price increases. One can conversely take a cynical stance, arguing that many of these customers will be transient relief workers or evacuees, so there is no need to fear loss of reputation with them. Also, local customers may have their mind on other pressing needs and so they may not notice or adversely react to price increases.

What levers can Reggie use to influence those who disagree with him?
It is this question that allows students to exercise their "ethics muscle" and normalize the stakes with respect to anticipated arguments in the previous

subsection. The market-based arguments in the preceding section are consistent with economists' regard for the price system as a superior method for coordinating economic activity. At the same time, students may be surprised to find that a large economics literature exists that supports the holding (or lowering) of prices of necessary goods in the aftermath of a natural disaster.[5] As not raising prices is the observed norm, this is why people are so outraged when prices are raised substantially and such instances become widely known.

With respect to the shortage that is expected to be generated at prices that are below their equilibrium level, one can argue that the relevant post disaster time period for the functioning of market-clearing prices is a *Marshallian period* in the classic sense of Marshall's (1961) *Principles.* A Marshallian period is one in which supply has become (perfectly) price inelastic at the post disaster available quantity. Consequently, any increase in price generates profits but it has no reallocation effect. In particular, below-equilibrium prices do not produce a shortage; the market will still clear at the lower price as well. From this perspective, the analogy to a binding price ceiling is false. Moreover, to the extent that rationing is needed the evidence suggests that consumers ration themselves at the non-market-clearing price, rather than formal rationing being undertaken by the firm. Self-rationing implies that the demand curve shifts back to the left; a price increase need not be inevitable.

In terms of political economy, not raising prices is a marginal contribution toward the maintenance of the societal order, which is an even more valuable public good during times of disaster. That is, raising prices may be the first step toward a breakdown in pro-social behavior and not raising prices has a measurable marginal value in this instance. Reggie may not want to be the "weak link" that eliminates the collective good associated with social order. After disasters the marginal social benefit of not raising prices can outweigh the marginal cost. Related to this is the idea that a disaster lowers the price (opportunity cost) of altruistic behavior and so more altruistic behavior should occur. Another economic rationale that has been put forth is that not raising prices is a form of social insurance that many firms are willing to supply as part of their "social license to operate" during normal times.

Within this context, one can also consider the impact of a price increase on future revenues. The opportunity costs of not raising prices include forgoing short-term profits, but what are the opportunity costs of raising prices? Waffle House may lose the goodwill of the community if it increases its prices. (Home Depot has a policy of price freezes during a declared emergency for precisely such reasons.) No price increase will create a locus of loyalty once the crisis is over but a price increase could have the opposite effect. It might even shift Waffle House's demand curve to the left when normal times return.

Solidarity is another reason for not increasing prices. Waffle House can provide empathy and support that boosts the morale of the affected community. Waffle house should not be seen as taking advantage of customers during a natural disaster. Their prices are not only paid by customers, but also they are publicly observable by others and so provide a signal of Waffle House's solidarity with the community.

Students are familiar with the Golden Rule and this can also be used to argue against dramatic price increases. It is exploitative to take advantage of consumer's vulnerability in order to derive disproportionate profits to the firm, even if buyers benefit themselves by having access to the good at a higher price. One must avoid additional unnecessary suffering and taking advantage of those who face unfortunate circumstances.

What is your most powerful and persuasive response to the reasons and rationalizations you need to address? To whom should the argument be made? When and in what context?

Asking students to produce a more fully articulated argument by elaborating on a single point identified within the previous subsection allows for further development of a values perspective as complementary to the economic context of the Waffle House case. Responses will therefore depend on answers to the preceding questions, and it can be powerful to record them for additional use, both in practice and for future classes.

GVV Throughout the Semester

As courses such as intermediate microeconomics, managerial economics, and economics for MBAs are primarily driven by problem sets, I augment several problem sets throughout the semester with GVV cases. Students are asked to work in groups and provide three to five brief and self-explanatory answers each for the stakeholder, rationalizations, and levers questions; and to write up two double-spaced pages making their most powerful and persuasive argument. In particular, the Profit Maximization and Layoffs case can be assigned when profit maximization is covered, and the Product Safety and (Preemptive) Recalls for problem sets having to do with public goods or game theory (the case has a game theoretic appendix). Both of these cases contain examples of responses, which can be used to discuss the cases after students have turned their answers in. Given the perceived role of incentive pay in the current financial crisis I often use the Agency and Corporate Governance case as a capstone exercise.

At the time that students turn in the GVV assignment I usually ask them to bring two copies, one to turn in and the other to discuss. Once the problem sets are turned in, I discuss any questions the students may have and then we turn to the GVV case. I first solicit student responses to each question. I then follow up their responses to the question with my own responses, which include those that come with the case and others that I have accumulated over time from past homework assignments. It definitely helps to be prepared with some of your own answers in case you need to break the ice. The discussion and debate that stem from the combined collection of answers is something that students definitely enjoy.

More often than not, some students will ask about Milton Friedman's (1970) article, "The Social Responsibility of the Firm is to Increase Profits," and will bring this article up during class discussion. It pays to be familiar with the article and, when the time comes, to point out that once one reads beyond the title of the article Friedman states that:

> That responsibility (of corporate executives) is to conduct the business in accordance with their desires (of owners and employees), which generally will be to make as much money as possible *while conforming to the basic rules of the society, both those embodied in law and those embodied in ethical custom* (p. 33, emphasis added).

In addition, I point out that the former president of the National Association of Business Economists (NABE), Roy E. Moor (1987, p. 12), asserts that ethics are intertwined with economics in all markets because all markets are composed of transactions that involve implicit as well as explicit agreements and understandings between the parties. I then ask: Who better then to understand the trade-offs than an economist? GVV facilitates the articulation of trade-offs that might otherwise be ignored to the detriment of the firm.

Conclusion

Looking back at a decade often called "The Noughties" because it was bookended with severe economic and financial crises stemming from unprincipled behavior associated with dot.com/new economy corporations (ENRON, Global Crossing, WorldCom, etc.) and dubious financial "innovations" (liar loans, AAA-ratings for subprime CMOs, ABACUS, etc.) one wonders whether an approach to business ethics that is *in vivo* could make business ethics seem less far-afield from business/economic practice than has been the case for business-ethics-as-formal-training-in-normative-decision-making. Giving Voice to Values (GVV) is an example of such an approach. It employs cases that are rooted within economics/business as its point of departure and broadens the perspective by asking students to address three concerns: (a) What is at stake for the key parties, including those with whom one disagrees? (b) What are the main (nonethical) arguments that one is trying to counter? That is, what are the reasons and rationalizations that need to be addressed? and (c) What levers can be used to influence those who disagree with the ethical perspective?

The chapter presents a GVV case that can be used in any economics course that covers the comparative statics of market equilibrium (supply and demand) by examining the movement of prices (or lack thereof) of necessary goods in the aftermath of a natural disaster. In particular, it looks at the pricing decisions of Waffle House, a firm that is widely known for its disaster preparedness; so much so that FEMA maintains a "Waffle House Index." The particular strength of this case is that economic arguments exist that are for and against raising prices, and students can easily place themselves within the situation to make ethical arguments without the need for introducing any formal theories of normative decision making. As such, I have effectively used this and other GVV cases in economics courses with both undergraduates and executive MBAs.

I conclude with a sampling of student reaction given in the course evaluation about the use of four GVV cases as group assignments over the course of a semester in an upper level undergraduate managerial economics course:

GVV is another example of how this class emphasizes real-world scenarios.

GVV seems to be the perfect way to explore the qualitative side of economics.

I have no interest in ethics to be honest.

The cases are interesting and meld theory and the real world well.

GVV makes us be more proactive in approaching the course material.

GVV is helpful in seeing that the class is more than pure textbook material.

Ethics was something that I did not associate with economics prior to GVV.

GVV is a necessary part of our learning process that we have not seen before.

These comments are representative in that they capture the spectrum and degree to which similar comments were given on my course evaluations. Although it is unlikely that students will unanimously agree on the utility of any one topic within this course, what these comments make clear is that students see GVV as being complementary to economic subject matter and relevant for business decision making outside of the classroom.

CHAPTER 3

Teaching *Change Leadership* for Sustainable Business

Strategies from the "Giving Voice to Values" Curriculum

Christopher P. Adkins

Abstract

The shift to sustainable business practices is a change process, requiring individuals who can help reshape both the strategy and the daily decision making of the organization. The Giving Voice to Values (GVV) program offers an action-based curriculum in which students develop strategies and scripts for sustainability leadership. This chapter discusses the advantages and applications of using GVV in teaching sustainability in business contexts. Specific themes include: integrating GVV within a variety of course designs and theoretical frameworks, leading sustainable change by aligning individual and organizational values, fostering a sense of self-efficacy based on past experience and peer coaching, and practical strategies for change agency that address common sustainability challenges. These advantages are illustrated using specific exercises from the GVV curriculum, and supplemented by suggestions for integrating resources from the sustainable business literature.

Keywords

sustainability, sustainable business, leadership, change management, shared value, self-efficacy, decision making, curricular integration, peer coaching.

Author Biography

Christopher P. Adkins, PhD., is Executive Director of the Undergraduate Business Program at the College of William & Mary (Mason School of Business). His research and teaching integrate insights from cognitive neuroscience, behavioral economics and social psychology to enhance business decision-making, particularly in the areas of ethics, sustainability, and social entrepreneurship. Current research projects include: the role of emotional memory in ethical decision making, empathic stakeholder analysis for value creation, and the interaction of pro-social and pro-self dispositions and behavior in entrepreneurial settings. In his teaching, Chris has pioneered the application of the MBA-level Giving Voice to Values approach with undergraduates. With sustainability consulting firm Saatchi S, Chris led the first personal sustainability program at a university. He is the co-founder of the Corporate & College Collaborative for Sustainability, a partnership of business leaders, faculty and students for innovation in sustainability education. Chris holds a PhD. and B.A. from William & Mary, and a M.A. from Boston University.

Teaching Change Leadership for Sustainable Business: Strategies from the "Giving Voice to Values" Curriculum

In discussing the importance of sustainability for business organizations, the conversation ultimately must address the question of value: How will sustainability create value for the business, for shareholders, and for stakeholders? Fortunately, a range of sustainability models[1] have emerged in management education to answer this question, as well as case studies of organizations who have successfully integrated sustainability to create economic, social, and environmental value. While conceptual knowledge and practical examples are necessary, an essential piece of the puzzle is missing: change leadership for sustainability. In short, the shift to sustainable business is a change process, requiring individuals who can reshape both the strategy and the daily decision making of the organization.[2] Approaches to sustainability education may fall short if they do not include the strategies and skills that prepare leaders to address the obstacles likely to arise in integrating sustainability in a business organization.

The Giving Voice to Values (GVV) program offers an action-based curriculum where students develop the strategies and scripts for sustainability leadership. In this chapter, I discuss the advantages and applications of using GVV in teaching sustainability in business contexts. First, GVV complements a variety of course designs and theoretical frameworks. Second, GVV addresses the ambiguity surrounding sustainability by identifying shared values across the organization and individuals. Third, GVV fosters a sense of self-efficacy in leading for sustainability, rooted in each individual's past experience and supported through peer coaching. Fourth, GVV provides practical strategies for change agency that address common sustainability challenges. Throughout this chapter, I will illustrate these advantages with specific exercises from the GVV curriculum, and offer suggestions for integrating additional resources from the sustainable business literature.

Advantages of the GVV Approach in Teaching Sustainability Leadership

GVV Complements a Variety of Course Designs and Theoretical Frameworks

Faculty teaching sustainability in business may come from diverse disciplines, utilize different frameworks, and teach within various course designs. The GVV approach can be adapted to this range of expertise, models, and courses. Within business schools, an entire course may be dedicated to sustainable business, or sustainability may be integrated within other courses, such as business ethics, business and society, supply chain, marketing, organizational behavior, and change management. The GVV curriculum can be used in both approaches; by design, the GVV exercises and cases can be sequenced for multiple sessions or be singled out for a specific session. For example, a course on sustainable business may utilize a mix of cases, pulled from the GVV curriculum and from other sources. Regardless of the case source, GVV offers the action-based "Reasons and Rationalizations"[3] framework for case analysis, in which the conversation moves from analysis to action, extending the emphasis from not only what should be done, but also the specific steps and conversations that must occur for change to occur.

The emphasis on planning behavior and rehearsal for action within the course context is a particular strength of GVV, in terms of both flexibility and transferability. For example, GVV does not explicitly adopt one definition of sustainability, or a specific model (such as triple bottom line, natural step, living principles for design); however, GVV does offer a framework for how one understands and acts from one's values. Thus, faculty can use the sustainability framework that best fits with their discipline, industry context, and course design, then utilize GVV to emphasize how the values of that particular framework can be practiced in leading change within the case scenarios and organizational contexts.

The strategies for leading change for sustainability can be transferred to leading change in other contexts as well. For example, the importance of engaging allies, focusing on small steps of change, seeking win–win opportunities, and finding shared values that are consistent with the organization's mission are effective strategies for leading change for sustainability, as well as other change initiatives.

GVV Uses the Language of Shared Values as Opposed to the Language of Sustainability

In teaching sustainability, one begins with several challenges. First, the very term "sustainability" is ambiguous, evoking a mix of concepts and values to different people. This is particularly true in organizations where "sustainability" can be seen as a new trend to the boomer generation, while the millennial generation has grown up with the concept of sustainability both in their education and in the marketplace.[4] Second, sustainability requires a long-term perspective of value creation, while short-term thinking focused on quarterly earnings often drives business decisions. Lastly, sustainability can strike many as value-laden, and thus the term may suggest normative and ethical implications. Such explicit or even implicit suggestions can be perceived as "imposing one's values" and may trigger a defensive response, depending on how the proposed initiative resonates (or does not) with one's own values as well as those of the organization.

One might be tempted to address these challenges directly, either by explicitly clarifying the concept of sustainability or by building the business case for sustainability. Indeed, this is the strategy used in many textbooks and articles, and the educational context is an ideal place for discussing such ideas. Yet in the workplace, one often does not have the time to educate their co-workers or their managers about the meaning of "sustainability." For example, "sustainability" is often associated with "going green" and the practices of conserving resources and reducing waste. While these are included in the concept of sustainability, this definition is narrow, focused primarily on environmental sustainability. Such a mental schema may not intuitively include the ideas of economic sustainability or social sustainability.

If the very word "sustainability" runs the risk of confusion at best and intuitive resistance at worst, then avoiding the term may be advantageous. This is the strategy used by sustainability business thinker and entrepreneur Amory Lovins. When asked in an interview with MIT Sloan Management Review, "When audiences of organization leaders ask what you mean by 'sustainability,' what do you tell them?", he replied:

> The question wouldn't arise because I don't use the word ... "Sustainability" means so many things to so many people that it's pretty useless. There are various standard definitions you can quote (Brundtland, Forum for the Future, etc.), but none is generally accepted. But behind your question is the core of something very important: the idea that doing business as if nature and people were properly valued actually creates stunning competitive advantage. To put it another way, if capitalism is a productive use of and reinvestment in capital, we can't deal only with financial and physical capital—money and goods. We also need to productively use and reinvest in the two more valuable kinds of capital—people and nature.[5]

This response may be surprising from the author of *Natural Capitalism*[6] and the founder of the Rocky Mountain Institute; yet, Lovins recognizes the importance of finding common values that resonate with his audience. He understands that organizations may have limited knowledge and experience with sustainability, and thus the language of sustainability is likely to fall on deaf ears. Instead, Lovins embraces the language of his audience and reframes the conversation around a shared business value (the "productive use of and reinvestment of capital") with the ultimate goal of strategic competitive advantage for the business.

Lovins' approach is consistent with how Gentile speaks of values. While not ignoring the differences that exist across individuals, ideologies, and cultures, she emphasizes that we can find common ground when it comes to values and motivations: "Accepting this premise—that is, the existence of a short list of shared values and, therefore, the possibility of shared goals—enables us to both prioritize our differences and also to frame the most important ones in ways that are more likely to communicate and resonate with different audiences."[7]

To illustrate the idea of focusing on shared values, I have my students read Gentile's chapter on "Values"[8] in conjunction with Porter and Kramer's article "Creating Shared Value."[9] Gentile offers the individual perspective, highlighting the opportunity to find common values across cultures and contexts; Porter and Kramer offer the organizational perspective, highlighting the opportunity for business to create shared value across economic, social, and environmental dimensions. Applying these ideas to sustainable business shifts the focus from definitions and frameworks to identifying shared goals for both individuals and the organization. In essence, one aligns sustainability with the strategy of the organization and with the values of the individuals working within the organization. "The fundamental stance we are taking in the Giving Voice to Values approach is one of alignment, of moving *with* our highest aspirations and our deepest sense of who we wish to be, rather than a stance of coercion and stern judgment, or of moving *against* our inclinations."[10]

GVV Builds Self-efficacy That Is Rooted in Past Experience and Personal Strengths, and Enhanced Through Peer Coaching

When it comes to leading for sustainability in one's own organization, students may hesitate, thinking that they lack previous experience in leading sustainability initiatives, or fearing that their organizations will resist such changes as too costly or time consuming. Faculty can point to success stories of other leaders who have changed organizations; GVV suggests that students begin by examining their past experiences in leading from their values. This approach is rooted in the second assumption of GVV: *"I have voiced my values, at some points in my past."*[11] The "Tale of Two Stories"[12] offers an exercise for such reflection, where students examine those instances where they have experienced a values conflict, and recall an episode where they voiced their values and one where they did not. In teaching sustainability leadership, I adapt the "Tale of Two Stories" exercise so that the question focuses on episodes of leading change: "Describe a time in your work experience when you voiced your values to effectively lead change within your organization? Describe a time when you missed an opportunity to voice your values and lead change within your organization?" If working with a group of managers experienced in sustainability, one can be more specific: "Describe a time in your career when you voiced your values and effectively led change within your organization in the areas of sustainability or social impact?"

The essence of this exercise emerges in a closer examination of the episodes, where individuals explore their own motivations and rationalizations ("what motivated you to lead—or not lead—change within your organization") as well as the conditions that enabled or disabled their change leadership ("identify the conditions in the situation that made it easier or more difficult to lead change"). The goal is to identify the "enablers" within oneself and in organizational contexts that facilitate leading from one's values, as well as the "disablers" that weaken one's own resolve or pose organizational obstacles. As students reflect on these contrasting experiences, and as they share their stories with others, they see patterns in their own behavior, identify common organizational challenges, and uncover practical strategies for leading change in the face of such challenges. Students often are surprised to discover they have influenced change in their past. They see their own personal style in voicing their values, and the situations where this style is more and less effective. Hearing the stories of the peers is both inspiring and illuminating, for they see the range of styles and strategies used by others within various organizational contexts.

This exercise lays an essential foundation for future case discussions. The sharing of stories has, in effect, shown that voicing values is not only possible, but is normal, and has revealed specific strategies that have been effective in a variety of contexts. Faculty can reference these lessons throughout the course, reminding students of their own experiences in voicing values.

Within the context of sustainability, this exercise also enhances the confidence necessary for change agency. In my teaching, I explicitly refer to Bandura's concept of self-efficacy.[13] As students revisit their past experiences in voicing their values, they develop a sense of self-efficacy to counteract the limited power one feels within organizations. Having this foundation of self-efficacy is essential for future success, as Bandura describes:

> Perceived self-efficacy concerns people's beliefs in their capabilities to mobilize the motivation, cognitive resources, and courses of action needed to exercise control over events in their lives. There is a difference between possessing skills and being able to use them well and consistently under difficult circumstances. To be successful, one not only must possess the required skills, but also a resilient self-belief in one's capabilities to exercise control over events to accomplish desired goals.[14]

Gentile describes this process as "finding one's voice," where, through reflection on the past, practice for the future, and coaching from one's peers, one develops the skills and confidence for future scenarios of challenge.

The "Tale of Two Stories" exercise emphasizes two of the sources for increasing one's sense of efficacy: mastery experiences and modeling. Mastery experiences are not simply those episodes where one effectively met a particular challenge, but achievements that came through sustained efforts: "If people experience only easy successes, they come to expect quick results and are easily discouraged by failure. To gain a resilient sense of efficacy, people must have experience in overcoming obstacles through perseverant effort."[15] Such resiliency is essential for change leaders, particularly when one considers the commitment required for systems change in organizations. Modeling offers the advantage of "conveying to observers effective strategies for managing different situations."[16] Hearing the change stories of fellow students is only one way GVV incorporates modeling. Gentile also offers guidelines for peer coaching[17] where students can offer critical feedback on the proposed scripts for voicing one's values. These conversations, either facilitated by faculty or convened in small student groups, strengthen the individual's own style and expand the strategies available for effective problem solving.

GVV Provides a Pragmatic Framework of Stakeholder Analysis and Action Planning in Preparation for the Common Obstacles to Sustainable Practices in Organizations

Increasing self-efficacy is an important first step, yet further mastery and modeling are needed to lead change for sustainability. Students need to anticipate the common challenges one will face when advocating for sustainability, such as increased costs, the challenges of implementation to replace existing systems and practices, and the simple resistance that arises when any change is proposed. As faculty integrate cases into their courses, they can apply GVV's "reasons and rationalizations" framework,[18] a pragmatic approach to case analysis that deepens stakeholder thinking, anticipates obstacles, and focuses on individual action planning. In teaching sustainability, I apply this approach to the following case[19] from the GVV curriculum:

Felipe Montez is the newly hired Purchasing Director and Product Designer for a Spanish electronics company. Based on his previous experience in purchasing, Felipe suggested the company cut out their distributor in Hong Kong, and work directly with the factories in South China. This change was implemented, and in turn eliminated the distributor's mark-up (which was sometimes as high as 30%).

In the 27 year history of the company, no one had ever visited the factories until Felipe's visit. While some of the factories were clean and organized, the main factory that supplied his company's goods prompted multiple concerns for Felipe: young girls worked long hours without magnifying glasses, the factory lacked air conditioning, some workers regularly inhaled gases from melted lead, and the housing for workers lacked windows as well as running water.

While the factory in question was prized for its speed and quality of products, the social and environmental conditions were unacceptable. What should Felipe say and do next?

Faculty may note that this scenario differs from sustainability cases that emphasize the organizational point of view or describe how a company has effectively made the shift to sustainable practice. Rather, students find themselves in the middle of a change scenario, one where there are both immediate opportunities for impact as well as the need for systemic change in both an organization and an industry.

Providing this change context expands how students think of voicing their values. When faculty bring the GVV approach to their courses, students focus on what they are going to say in the immediate situation, to the individual or individuals right in front of them. As Gentile notes, however, voicing our values is not simply about what we say in one particular moment, but how we can lead and act over time, in a variety of situations, with a range of audiences. To emphasize the long view of change leadership, I have developed a "change agent approach" for GVV, as described in these presentation guidelines for my student teams:

When you think of "giving voice to your values," you may think about what you are going to say in the situation right in front of you. Often the current situation has deeply rooted causes that extend beyond the present challenge. In such cases, raising your voice is not only about what you say in the "short-term" to address immediate concerns, but it is about developing a "long-term" strategy that will address the deeper issues.

This week, we want to practice "voicing our values" to foster real and sustainable change. In other words, we want to explore how you become a change agent, from your initial actions (how you first speak up) to your future actions (how you will continue to voice your values in future conversations and actions).

In your presentation, you are advising Felipe Montez on how he can become a change agent by "giving voice to his values" in both the short and long term. You will need to present him (and our class) with: 1) a *script* of the "most powerful and persuasive response" he should *vocalize* in the short-term; 2) a strategic plan of *actions* for following up on this first response that will lead *to deeper and systemic change.*

In preparing the case, the student team applies the reasons and rationalizations framework, first identifying the mix of arguments that Felipe will need to address, both in his own mind and with key stakeholders. Students tend to easily identify the disablers: the potential increase in cost and timeliness of production, the well-established nature of the factory practices, the suggestion that factory conditions offer a higher quality of work than other labor opportunities in the area. The enablers are more difficult to see, considering the scope of such a challenge and the established practices of both the organization and the industry. To prompt solutions, we return to the strategies that have emerged throughout the course, including the "Tale of Two Stories" reflection and other case discussions. We also revisit the enablers[20] Gentile offers in her text, and focus on those strategies suited for sustainability change:

> ***Playing to one's strengths.*** Students often overlook the credibility Felipe has in this scenario. Soon after joining the company, he became a positive change agent, immediately saving the company significant costs by eliminating the distributor and the associated mark-up costs. What strategies did he use in getting this proposal approved, and how might he use a similar approach in the current situation? Also, how might he use this early success as leverage in proposing changes in factory conditions?
>
> ***Incremental steps.*** In developing their response, students see immediate opportunities for impact, such as magnifying glasses and sterile masks. Felipe's boss indicated that he is open to these changes, and these changes may be important incremental steps or early wins that will build momentum for other changes. For example, the magnifying glasses may improve production quality and speed; if so, these positive results can be used in conversations with the factory manager, his own supervisor, and the other companies who use the factory to advocate for additional investments that enhance working conditions and efficiency of production.

Engaging allies. The more challenging issues, such as the working conditions in the factory and the living conditions of the workers, require a significant commitment of leadership and resources from his organization, the cooperation of the factory manager, and support from other factory clients. Felipe can focus on building relationships with these decision makers. He can also identify those who have influence over these decision makers, and engage them as allies.

Beginning with questions. Students often suggest a conversation with the factory manager, where Felipe threatens to withdraw support of the factory unless conditions change. This may be necessary at some point, but before putting their current supply chain at risk, Felipe can begin by simply asking questions. First, he can ask the factory manager questions about the working and living conditions, if they have always been this way, if efforts have been made to improve the conditions, and what challenges the manager would encounter in trying to improve the conditions. With his boss and his peers who also rely on the factory, Felipe can explore the rationale and the history of using this particular factory, and if alternative sources have been explored.

Understanding others' concerns and fears. Through these questions, Felipe will begin to understand the reasons and rationalizations of the other stakeholders. Felipe will hear firsthand the concerns of others, as opposed to projecting his own ideas of the obstacles ahead. Such insights will clarify the difficulties he is likely to face when proposing changes. The conversations also build trust and respect with key stakeholders, and thus solidify the foundation for effective working relationships.

Reframing challenge as opportunity. In his conversations, Felipe may uncover that the challenges can be reconsidered as opportunities to create value. For example, if the concern is increased costs, the improvements can be reframed as cost-saving opportunity: by minimizing safety risks and reducing physical strain, quality of work and speed of production will increase.

Selecting and sequencing audiences. "Who should Felipe approach first? Why" This simple question is essential in helping the students think as change agents. Who they choose and why reveals their intent: Are they focused on gathering more information, engaging an ally and building relationships, achieving an early win? Students will offer a mix of responses and rationales, and faculty can facilitate this discussion to emphasize the importance of having a plan for change. I ask my students to work backward from the desired outcome, and then identify the conversations, information, and buy-in needed from key stakeholders to accomplish this goal. In this case, if a team seeks to improve the air quality of the factory, the factory manager, his own supervisor and other clients will be concerned about a reduction in the production speed while the proposed changes are implemented (not to mention the costs of such changes). At the very least, Felipe will need a plan that estimates costs and identifies alternative suppliers for the implementation period before he can rally the support of his boss and ideally other clients for such a change.

Appealing to organizational policies, legal obligations, and industry standards. Felipe's company, not to mention the other clients of the factory, will be concerned by the costs associated with the changes. Such costs can be framed as necessary to avoid legal and reputational risks. Felipe can appeal to the policies of his own organization, as well as those of his industry, regarding working conditions for employees. He can research the legal requirements of labor practices that apply to this scenario. He also can highlight the criticisms his own company will face for allowing such conditions. In my courses, we discuss Zadek's article[21] on Nike's failures to effectively address factory conditions, and the consequences for the company.

In addition to Gentile's strategies, I propose an additional strategy: leveraging the power of proximity so that the decision makers experience the problem firsthand. One aspect of the case that students often overlook is the fact that Felipe is the first one to visit any of the factories in the company's 27-year history. Moreover, not all of the factories had significant concerns. What does this mean for Felipe, for the others in his organization, and for the other clients of the factory? Felipe was not aware of the problem, nor did he feel the urgency of addressing the problem, until he experienced the conditions firsthand. He can try to communicate his experience, but his efforts will lack the emotional power and urgency that comes from personal experience. In driving change, it is important that the key decision makers experience the problems themselves. Within the context of sustainability, this is particularly important, for the implications often are not immediately present. As Kotter and Cohen[22] propose, problems must be both seen and felt before the need for change becomes real. For my students, I emphasize the power of proximity, so that the problem becomes visual and visceral, experienced up close and personal.

For Felipe, this means developing a strategy where the key decision makers—his superiors and his peers at other organizations—visit this factory so they experience what he has seen. Moreover, they need to see the contrast of this factory with the other factories who have better working conditions. Felipe could orchestrate such a visit of several factories for key decision makers in his organization within the context of improving their supply chain. For his peers in other organizations, he can frame the visit around due diligence or best practices in manufacturing.

Building from this mix of strategies, students develop action plans and specific scripts for the first conversations needed to prompt change. Students may begin with the factory manager, Felipe's own supervisor, his peers at other companies, or perhaps others in the organizations. In each instance, students must focus not only on voicing the value of sustainability, but also speaking in such a way that their message resonates with the values of the individual across the table.

Preparing for the Challenge of Sustainability Leadership

Throughout their careers, our students will find themselves in a variety of organizational contexts, leading from a variety of roles. In teaching sustainability for business, theoretical understanding must be accompanied by best practices in values-based leadership. The GVV program provides this emphasis on change leadership for sustainability, offering a curriculum that can easily be adapted to different course designs and sustainability models. As challenges emerge in course texts, case studies, or even in the experiences of the students, GVV offers specific exercises and frameworks to prepare for such challenges. In developing responses, faculty can leverage the styles of each student to expand the mix of perspectives and strategies available in leading change for sustainability. This mix of voices, balanced by readings and cases in sustainability and change management, creates a learning environment where conceptual understanding is linked to best practices in leading for change.

CHAPTER 4

Giving Voice to Values in Accounting Education

Steven M. Mintz and Roselyn E. Morris

Abstract

Ethics education of accounting students traditionally has focused on the application of reasoning methods to resolve ethical dilemmas but it stops short of providing a way to resolve conflicts when professional and personal values conflict. The Giving Voice to Values (GVV) approach provides a framework to identify the factors and people who might enable a decision maker to speak up when those values conflict and the tools to counteract those who make it more difficult to voice values. Through short cases and role-play experiences, we explain how the GVV approach is used in our accounting classes to help students better understand ways to get their point across and effect change.

Keywords

accounting ethics education, earnings expectations, expense reimbursement, internal accounting environment, professional accounting values, year-end accruals.

Author Biography

Steven Mintz received his doctorate from The George Washington University. Dr. Mintz is professor of Accounting in the Orfalea College of Business at the California Polytechnic State University in San Luis Obispo. He has an international reputation for his research in ethics and teaching accounting ethics. Dr. Mintz has coauthored (with Roselyn Morris) the accounting ethics textbook: *Ethical Obligations and Decision Making in Accounting: Text and Cases.* Dr. Mintz has published more than 20 research papers in accounting and business ethics. He has made dozens of presentations to professional and academic groups on accounting ethics and is frequently interviewed for his perspective on ethics issues.

Roselyn Morris received her PhD from the University of Houston. Dr. Morris is professor of Accounting in the McCoy College of Business Administration at Texas State University—San Marcos. She has a national reputation for teaching and designing accounting ethics courses to comply with state board of accountancy requirements. Dr. Morris has coauthored (with Steven Mintz) the accounting ethics textbook: *Ethical Obligations and Decision Making in Accounting: Text and Cases.* Dr. Morris has published more than 15 research papers in auditing and accounting ethics. She has made numerous presentations to academic groups on her research and the teaching of accounting ethics.

Giving Voice to Values in Accounting Education

Introduction and Background

By certifying the public reports that collectively depict a corporation's financial status, the independent auditor assumes a public responsibility transcending any employment responsibility with the client. The independent public accountant performing this special function owes ultimate allegiance to the corporation's creditors and stockholders, as well as to the investing public. This 'public watchdog' function demands that the accountant maintain total independence from the client at all times and requires complete fidelity to the public trust (United States v. Arthur Young [465 U.S. 805 (1984)]).

This seminal ruling by the US Supreme Court reminds us that the independent audit provides the foundation for the existence of the accounting profession in the United States. Accounting is the only business profession (the licensed certified public accountants) where the public interest is placed ahead of the interests of an employer, client, or one's own self-interest. The accounting profession's public consists of clients, credit grantors, governments, employers, investors, the business and financial community, and others who rely on the objectivity and integrity of CPAs to maintain the orderly functioning of commerce. These are the stakeholders of the profession.

The Code of Professional Conduct of the American Institute of CPAs (AICPA) establishes that the Public Interest Principle is the foundation of the profession. External auditors are expected to render an opinion whether the financial statements are free of material misstatements that may be due to error, illegal acts, and fraud. Internal accountants and auditors have ethical obligations in their role of preparing and examining their employer's financial statements that include objectivity and integrity. The integrity standard is critical in accounting and it provides that an accountant should not subordinate professional judgment to that of a client or one's employer. The public places its trust in the accounting profession to safeguard the entity's resources and detect financial statement fraud.

The most challenging issues for accountants and auditors occur when conflicts of interest exist among stakeholder groups. For example, top management of an employer may pressure accountants to go along with materially false or misleading financial statements, or the external auditor may be pressured by a client to accept these reports even though they do not comply with generally accepted accounting principles.[1] In such cases, established professional values should guide decisions about what is the right thing to do. A good example is the Integrity Principle (AICPA 2012, ET Section 54) that provides guidance on dealing with conflicts and raises important questions that help determine what to do in a conflicting situation.

> Integrity is measured in terms of what is right and just. In the absence of specific rules, standards, or guidance, or in the face of conflicting opinions, a member should test decisions and deeds by asking: "Am I doing what a person of integrity would do? Have I retained my integrity?" Integrity requires a member to observe both the form and the spirit of technical and ethical standards;

circumvention of those standards constitutes subordination of judgment.

The application of ethical principles to a fact situation depends on being able to voice one's values when pressures exist to do otherwise. The values of the accounting profession include honesty, integrity, trustworthiness, due care, responsibility and accountability.

Traditional ethics education in accounting emphasizes the application of ethical reasoning in a decision-making framework but does not allow for responses when professional and personal values conflict. This chapter will discuss conflict situations in accounting and the use of Giving Voice to Values (GVV) to counter arguments by developing persuasive responses in role-play situations. We discuss using GVV in an accounting classroom, give two examples of GVV cases, and discuss implementation challenges to students and faculty in incorporating GVV in an accounting classroom. This chapter will conclude with the benefits of incorporating GVV.

Using GVV in the Classroom

We use the GVV framework in the classroom to complement discussions of professional accounting values. Typically, accounting professors rely on the use of traditional moral theories to provide the basis for value judgments. The problem is the discussion of what to do stops there and not with the critical issue of how to do it and be true to one's values. We use the GVV approach to provide the bridge between ethical intent and ethical action. The idea is to provide students with the tools to deal with questionable accounting and financial reporting treatments by developing arguments to bring to discussions with those who disagree with one's point of view.

In our experience, accounting students most often know what to do but may not feel comfortable doing it. This is where we rely on the GVV rubric to let students know that despite the risks and complexities of ethically challenging situations, they can speak up about their values and take effective action.[2] We encourage students to think about factors or persons that encourage them to act on their values—enablers—and those that discourage them, or serve as disablers. Students learn strategies to strengthen enablers and counteract the disablers. They grow surer of themselves each time they speak up. GVV shifts the focus away from debates about what is the "right" answer to an ethical challenge and places the focus on how to act on one's values in a particular situation.

We use GVV in basic and advanced accounting courses at the undergraduate and graduate levels. One advantage of the technique is the facts and circumstances of the case situation can change to meet course content but the approach is the same. We introduce GVV by asking students to reflect on a situation they faced where their values conflicted with what they were asked to do.

We find that students sometimes are reluctant to share their experiences and innermost thoughts and feelings so we come to class prepared with an example to illustrate a typical conflict between one's values and organizational expectations. The following is an example of a case we use early on in a course to introduce the GVV technique.

The Personal Expense Reimbursement Case

Expense reimbursements are fertile areas for fraud, no matter the industry. The 2012 Global Fraud Study published by the Association of Certified Fraud Examiners (ACFE), *Report to the Nations on Occupational Fraud and Abuse*, reports that 5 percent of revenues of organizations are lost to fraud and embezzlements each year.[3] The most common type of occupational fraud is asset misappropriation, comprising 87 percent of the cases reported to the ACFE. Eight of nine categories of asset misappropriation involve the misuse of cash with the most common being billing schemes (24.9%) where employees submit invoices for purchases of personal items or inflate expenditure requests for reimbursement such as for travel expenses.

The ACFE report found that expense reimbursements accounted for 5.7 percent of the fraud in the banking and financial services industry (the low end) to 31.5 percent of the fraud in religious and charitable organizations (the high end).[4] The latter is primarily due to poor internal controls and trusting individuals with bookkeeping and financial reporting responsibilities in part because of the nature of the mission of charitable organizations.

Our example involves the story of Troy who just returned from a business trip for health care administrators in Orlando. Troy works for a for-profit hospital in the St. Louis area. Javier, the insurance claims director for the hospital, also attended the conference. The Orlando conference included training in the newest regulations over health care and insurance, networking with other hospital administrators, and reports on upcoming legislation in health care. The conference was in early March and matched the Troy kids' school spring break so the entire family traveled to Orlando.

The hospital's expense reimbursement policy is very clear on the need for receipts for all reimbursements. Meals, for those not included in the conference, are covered within a preset range. Troy has never had a problem following those guidelines. However, the trip to Orlando was more expensive than Troy expected. He did not attend all sessions of the conference to enjoy time with the family. On return to St. Louis, Troy's spouse suggested that Troy submit three meals and one extra night at the hotel as business expenses when they are personal expenses. The rationale was that the hospital policies would not totally cover the business costs of the trip. Troy often has to travel and misses family time that cannot be recovered or replaced. Troy also knows his boss has a reputation of signing forms without reading or careful examination.

Megan is the staff accountant who handles travel reimbursements for the hospital. Javier hands in his receipts and the program for the conference on his return so that the travel reimbursement could be worked up. Knowing that Troy was also attending the conference, Megan works his reimbursement, just needing the airplane receipts, and other incidental receipts. The next day Troy takes his receipts to Megan, and says that he does not have the program but he was in Orlando for five nights (rather than the four nights that Javier showed). Megan mentions that she has the program and was just waiting on Troy's receipts. Megan asks Troy to wait as she enters his receipts and then he can review and sign the travel voucher for reimbursement. Troy notices that Megan includes four nights, not the five that he was claiming. He looks further and notices that the three extra meals he was claiming were not included. Troy asks why all of his expenses were not included. Megan explains that the conference only required four nights in Orlando and that the meals he claimed were provided by the conference. Troy becomes upset and presses Megan to include all the nights and meals that he requested. He asks Megan to bend the rules this once. How should Megan respond? Put yourself in Megan's shoes and consider each of the following four questions and write down your thoughts, feelings, and brief responses:

- What would motivate you to speak up and act or to stay silent?
- What are the arguments you are trying to counter?
- What would you do and who would you speak to?
- What do you hope will happen and what will you do if it does not?

What would motivate you to speak up and act or to stay silent?
We want students to get in touch with their feelings and personalize the matter. Do they feel a loyalty obligation to Troy or the hospital? How should Megan feel about being asked to bend the rules for a co-worker? What are their responsibilities to the hospital? We also expect students to address the expense reimbursement policy and whether one employee should be allowed to deviate from the policy for any reason while others comply. The students are encouraged to voice their values and lead the situation to the ethical solution.

What are the arguments you are trying to counter?
Here students address the issue that it is common for employees to inflate expense reports with seemingly no consequences. Megan needs to deal with the "everybody does it" and "don't rock the boat culture" that implies you need to go along to get along in the organization. Students come to realize that the way they handle the situation will set the tone for whether they act on their values or allow others to dictate how to handle the situation.

What would you do and who would you speak to?
We ask students to consider what steps they might take, people to talk to, and come to a decision what action is appropriate given Troy's request. We find this question can be the most challenging for students. Most students point to their relationships with co-workers as the determining

factor whether they would speak up and act or stay silent. If they feel intimidated by Troy, then they look to their boss or the accounting head to back them up in the situation. Students often want to know what the reporting lines and job titles are before responding. They often base their answer on past job experiences of their own and whether their boss supported them or not. The strength of the exercise is to help the students to be part of the decision-making process in a positive role. The practice will help them prepare and empower the students for a real situation.

We find that the students want Megan to remain firm in her position to follow the policies of the hospital. Many want Megan to seek the help from the accounting head to back her up. Others want to use that approach only as a last resort. We took this opportunity to role-play the discussion between Megan and Troy. We asked each student group to select one member to play the role of Megan and the other Troy. We repeated the exercise with two teams to see if the interaction between the students in each group led to a different outcome. The results of the two teams were the same in the end, but the approach of each team was very different. In the first team Megan was able to convince Troy that the calculated reimbursement was correct using the conference program and schedule of meetings and the hospital policy on reimbursements. The second team still found a values-driven solution for Megan but this time Troy was much more insistent on the additional hotel night and meals. This team had the discussion expanded to include Javier and the accounting head before Troy would acquiesce to the reduced reimbursement.

Students note that they were glad that Megan did not directly report to Troy. The students discuss how uncomfortable the situation would have been if Troy had been Megan's boss (the next case does have the student role-play taking a stand against higher ups in an organization). The first team assumed that the travel reimbursement policies were written and published policies available to all employees, not just a verbal policy between the accounting department personnel. The second team did not assume that the policies were necessarily published and allowed Troy to use that fact as a pressure on Megan to go along with him. In the class discussion it was noted and finally understood that written and published accounting policies can be a strong internal control that enables accounting personnel to be firm and consistent in application.

What do you hope will happen and what will you do if it does not?
This question is a follow-up to the previous one so students' responses differ on the basis of what they would do in the role play and who they would speak to. In discussing the situation in the class we make an assumption about what has happened and ask students to react. We have used this case in the class as a written, hand-in assignment and as a class discussion with role-play. The written assignment focuses on ethical reasoning and tends to lead students to do an analysis using consequentialism. The cost–benefit analysis that students do suffers from not incorporating the human element that is so important in expressing one's values. It inhibits the give-and-take of real-life ethical decision making that is supported by role-playing exercises. Students sometimes miss the point that regardless of any utilitarian benefits, certain acts should not be taken because they violate basic principles of right and wrong.

Internal Accounting Environment and Decision Making

Some of the most difficult ethical conflicts in accounting occur at the internal environment level. Internal accountants and auditors might be pressured by superiors to accept improper accounting in order to meet financial analysts' earnings estimates, increase stock prices and enhance shareholder value, and maximize executive compensation including bonuses and stock options. The challenge for accountants is to place the public interest ahead of one's own self-interests and the interests of a supervisor and one's employer.

In the past, we have discussed such situations with students using a decision-making model that incorporates professional accounting values and ethics with virtue considerations and ethical reasoning methods. The approach builds on Rest's Model of Moral Development as follows.[5]

Moral sensitivity or the ability to interpret a situation as moral;

Moral judgment or the ability to apply prescriptive reasoning to think through an ethical conflict and decide what ought to be done;

Moral motivation or being willing (ethical intention) to place ethical values such as honesty, integrity, and trustworthiness ahead of nonethical values such as wealth, power, and fame that relate to self-interest; and

Moral character or having the courage to carry through ethical intent with ethical action (integrity).

The decision-making model is as follows.

1. **Identify the ethical and professional issues (Ethical Sensitivity)**
   What are the ethical and professional issues in this case (i.e., accounting and auditing standards)?
   Who are the stakeholders (i.e., shareholders, creditors, employees)?
   Which accounting, auditing, and ethical standards apply (i.e., AICPA Code)?

2. **Identify the alternative courses of action (Ethical Judgment)**
   What can and cannot be done in resolving the conflict under professional standards?
   Which ethical reasoning methods apply to help reason through alternatives (i.e., rights theory, utilitarianism, virtue)?

3. **Incorporate core professional values, ethics, and attitudes to motivate ethical action (Ethical Intent)**
   Consider how virtue considerations (i.e., moral virtues) motivate ethical actions
   Consider how AICPA standards (i.e., independence, objectivity, integrity, professional skepticism) motivate ethical actions and behaviors

4. **Decide on a course of action (Ethical Behavior)**
   Consider your ethical responsibilities as a professional accountant
   Which action best meets the public interest obligation
   How can virtue considerations (i.e., instrumental virtues) support turning ethical intent into ethical action?
   What will you do and why?

We have found that accounting faculty feel comfortable using such a decision-making model because it clearly defines the steps students should take to resolve the dilemma and the factors to consider along the way. This rigid approach is consistent with the notion that the accounting process is inflexible and does not lend itself to creative decision making (not to be confused with creative accounting). Yet, in the real world, even accounting matters are not cut and dry and often are resolved through the give-and-take process of deliberation, argumentation, and responses that are part of the GVV framework.

When we use the model for a written individual case assignment we hear from students that they find it to be a sterile approach and feel like they have to respond in a certain way to meet their professor's expectations. They feel constrained by the four-step model that does not allow for interaction with their fellow students. They feel compelled to go along with the flow and lack the ability to communicate to superiors as to why they feel a certain course of action is the right one. Even when used in a role-play context, the students feel the model creates barriers that make it difficult to communicate in an effective way and to counteract the reasons and rationalizations given by a superior for a specific course of action.

The Year-End Accrual Case

At the end of a year the accountant looks at various unrecorded expenses and liabilities (reserves) and any reversals and determines how to adjust the financial statements for accrued amounts. These entries are necessary to bring the books and records up to date prior to the preparation of the financial statements. The internal auditors review such entries prior to the external audit by independent accountants. The entries are critical to a fair presentation of the financial results and to ward off the temptation to manage earnings because unsubstantiated entries or arbitrary reversals of accruals can be used to smooth net income motivated by the desire to meet financial analysts' earnings estimates, and/or enhance share value thereby making stock options more valuable.

Our case deals with a situation where accrual entries are made after the year end that reduces reserve balances and increases income. It involves Sandy Cole, the director of the internal auditing department at Dunco Industries, a publicly owned company with operations in seven countries around the world. Sandy just completed her review of various accrual accounts in connection with the year-end internal audit of the company's financial statements. She uncovered 10 manual entries made after the quarter's close that lacked sufficient supporting documentation and that significantly reduced the reserve balance for each account. Sandy reviewed the entries in the system and found the same explanation for each reduction: "reduce accrual by $1.5 million, per Jim Benson, corporate controller." The total amount of reductions came to $15 million, a material amount to the financial statements of Dunco.

Sandy goes to see Jim Benson and expresses her concern about the 10 entries and lack of supporting documentation. Benson tells her the entries have been approved but skirts around Sandy's question whether they have been approved by Harry Stone, the chief financial officer. Instead, Sandy is told that pressure exists within the company to do all that is necessary to increase earnings for the year to meet financial analysts' earnings expectations and maximize share price and bonuses. Benson goes on to explain that the company has been struggling due to competition from abroad and rumors are circulating that the company may move its operations overseas to be more competitive with labor costs and increase profitability of its product lines.

At this point Sandy is not sure what to do. The meeting ends when Benson informs Sandy the internal audit report must be completed by the end of the week because the external auditors are coming in next week to begin their year-end examination of the company's financial statements. Benson closes by telling Sandy that she doesn't want to push back on the accrual issue at this late stage as it will surely lead to problems with the external auditors.

We ask students to consider the following as we review the case in class:

- Identify the stakeholders of the case and what is at stake.
- Identify the main arguments you are trying to counter.
- Describe three solutions/approaches you considered.
- Identify your most effective and persuasive response of the three and describe this response in detail.

We also tell students they may want to include the "approach" for the response they develop to act out in the role-play during class. In the past, when we have used the decision-making model in a written assignment, the students say all the "right" things; they follow the profession's standards for discussing matters of concern with superiors and take the matter all the way up to the board of directors if necessary. In a role-play situation, we ask each team to act out their case and their preferred response and approach in class. We allow them to expand or change the characters and details of the case as they wish to make it their own, but not to change the main issue of the case. Students are told to present a clear solution to the main issue that is easy for their fellow classmates to identify. They must solve the dilemma, not just set up the different solutions. All members of the group must participate in the same way and one can be a "narrator."

We proceed with the role-play in one of two ways. The first is to have the student playing the role of Sandy begin by discussing the matter with whomever one chooses—Benson or Stone, for example. They play out their chosen response and another student reacts from the perspective of Benson or Stone. The role-play takes its own course and the other characters are added as decided by the group. For example, if Sandy is told by Benson and Stone that the accruals will be made regardless of what she says, then Sandy might approach the external auditors since she knows they rely on the work of the internal accountants and auditors in performing the external audit. Furthermore, she knows the underlying motivation to reverse the accruals is to make the earnings look better than they really are and while such a practice might be acceptable if it had involved the choice of an accounting policy, it is not proper in this instance because the intent is to manipulate (manage) earnings. Another character joins the discussion that may take place between Sandy and the external auditor(s). We have found this to be a common direction for the role-play as most students find approaching the external auditors as the most powerful and persuasive response.

The other way we move forward with the case is to start with Sandy going to see Benson and questioning him about the 10 entries. This tends to work well in a role-play situation because Benson's response changes depending on how Sandy approaches him, and Sandy's reaction is effected in turn. In one instance, the group decided that Sandy would suggest setting up a meeting with Harry Stone, Benson's boss. The discussion that ensued between Sandy and Benson got heated at times; it could not be duplicated in a written assignment. The goal is not an adversarial role-play, but an exploration of the pressures and approaches to achieve an ethical outcome. Students are often very hesitant to suggest going over their supervisor's head and do not want to take the matter outside the company or even to the external auditors. Students may want clarification on whether Sandy's boss is Jim Benson, Harry Stone, or the audit committee of the board of directors. Class analysis and discussion after the role play can consider when and how to take concerns up the organization ladder or to the audit committee. The students have noted that these considerations have shown that they do have some options and do not have to go along with pressures or unethical situations. Students note that they would prefer that Sandy report directly to the audit committee rather than to Benson or Stone. This analysis helps the students understand and respond to pressures and veiled threats of "you are not a team player," "this will be reflected in your next evaluation," or even "your job is on the line." Class discussion often then turns to how to respond and contingency plans when the job is on the line.

We have found that in some role-plays as students become actors, they may not end up with the ideal solution or may act out Benson bullying Sandy in the skit. Students tell us that acting out the part requires thinking, walking, and so many activities at once that the solution may not come as originally planned. If the role-play goes into bullying or not as strong an ethical solution as the ideal, the class analyzes how to "rewind" to the play so that Sandy is successful in voicing her values and coming to a values-driven solution.

Since we assign a different case to each group for role-play purposes, the other teams are asked to respond to the aforementioned four requirements in a written assignment that is handed in before the role play. After the role play, we ask each team to hand in what they would have done differently from Sandy.

Another way to involve the nonperforming students is to assign an in-class reflection exercise where each student fills out a reflection worksheet during the case presentations. Students are asked to read each of the cases and identify the main issue in the case prior to class. During the presentation each student is asked to write down: (a) how each group addressed the issue; (b) what would have been their solution if they had performed the role-play; and (c) how effective was the solution as portrayed by the students in the role-play? These items are rated on a scale of one (not effective) to five (extremely effective). Each student is also asked to make suggestions for the group. The ratings and suggestions are then discussed in class to provide feedback to each group for their next role-play presentation.

Challenges (or Logistics) to Implementing GVV in a Classroom

Asking accountants to emote sounds like an oxymoron. It is one of the biggest challenges for a faculty member using GVV cases. Since the faculty member cannot see herself acting out a case without a detailed, planned script (and maybe not even then), she hesitates to ask students to do such a case. The faculty may also hesitate to use a case that does not indicate the ethical solution. However, one of the greatest benefits from using a GVV case is that students must determine how to achieve an ethical solution in agreement with their values to that situation. In advanced accounting or graduate classes the nuances of different accounting methods may have different ethical solutions. Students may need help in recognizing the ethical implications of the different accounting methods or judgments. Once the students realize those implications, the solutions become clearer to the students. Then the students work on finding an effective approach to achieve that solution. Another hesitation by the faculty to implementing GVV cases is how to grade, assess, or control the use of the case in the classroom.

Many students, by contrast, seem to enjoy the opportunity to be creative and act out a scenario, even without getting a grade for the assignment. (Many students are secret aspiring directors and actors, or may just want to get on YouTube! Some shyer students hesitate at first but then get into the spirit of the role-play). As students get into the role-play, they often add costuming, props, cameo roles, and subtext drama. Students have commented that the subtext drama helps make the situation seem real and something that might happen in reality. A student commented that, "Acting out the scenario made me feel the pressure to give in to my supervisor even when I knew that was the wrong course of action. Following my supervisor's directions can seem like the right thing to do even when it was the wrong thing to do." One student commented that after being part of the role-play, "I will not be so judgmental of the Betty Vinson's of the world following the controller's or CFO's instructions."

(Betty Vinson was an accountant at WorldCom who made fraudulent entries to keep her job, benefits, and provide for her family). The exercise helps train the students to develop a practical, effective, and ethical solution when faced with the pressures like Betty Vinson.

The students develop their scripts for the cases. For example, in scripting the aforementioned "The Personal Expense Reimbursement Case," some teams will want to script only the three main characters of Troy, Javier, and Megan. Most teams enjoy being able to do a scene with Troy and his wife setting up the workplace discussion. Then students may add other members of the hospital to interact with Megan, Javier, and Troy. Some students also like to add a scene with other friends out of the work place to act as sounding boards to the planned action. Some students may add the subtext that Troy's wife is expecting, that Javier did not take his family due to an ill family member, or that Megan is working to save for her wedding.

Another challenge to implementing GVV is class time and size. One of the coauthors uses three different approaches to overcome those challenges. The class time has been solved by determining groups and assigning cases a week before the actual role play. The students are given an hour of class time to discuss who is doing what in the team, assign roles, and set up any other meeting times. Some teams script entire plays; other set up different acts and general direction of the play without detailed scripts, allowing the students to ad lib as the action unfolds.

To solve the class size challenge, one approach is to have two to three teams act out the scenario. The rest of the class writes memos to a supervisor (or arguing against) the position of the main player in the ethical dilemma. Students comment that having to craft responses to pressures to act unethically strengthens their resolve to act in an ethical or values-true manner in reality. When the class size was still too large to have all students on teams, some students were judges of the different teams. In an upcoming term, the teams will be taped and used as an example of the role-play for future classes.

Assessment and grading of the role play is the same as an oral presentation with a team evaluation. So far the teams note that all members pull their weight as the assignment is so much fun and creative. Some aspects of the assessment include values voiced, resolution of the dilemma, and understandability of the scripts and actors. Students appreciate creativity being recognized in the assessment or grading. If students act as judges, those students are peer assessors, justify their rankings, and appreciate the insight into grading and assessing.

Benefits of Implementing GVV

The students benefit from using GVV cases and gain experience in recognizing ethical dilemmas, resisting pressure to act in a certain way, and a safe environment to learn responses to those pressures. The students, who act out as the co-worker pressuring a co-worker or a subordinate, comment on the discomfort felt being in that role, and also becoming more aware of subtle pressure of peers or supervisors to act against personal values. Those students comment on resolve to support peers in difficult situations in the future. Students comment on the difference between writing about ethics cases and being part of a GVV role-play is the ability to know and voice values while carrying on dialogues. It takes the learning experience from a passive activity to an active resolve to improve character and remain true to values.

CHAPTER 5

Giving Voice to Values in Human Resource Management Practice and Education

Charmine E. J. Härtel and Amanda Roan

Abstract

In this chapter we explore how GVV can be embedded in a Human Resource Management (HRM) curriculum. We begin by showing how we place HRM in an ethics context by emphasizing the advantages of developing a positive workplace environment (PWE) where people can perform to the best of their abilities and express and act on their personal values. Following discussion of the concept of PWE and how we introduce it to the classroom, we provide teaching notes and four examples of case studies where GVV is applied.

Keywords

Human Resource Management, workplace climate, ethics education, values, employee voice.

Author Biography

Dr. Charmine E. J. Härtel is Head of Management and Chair of Human Resource Management and Organizational Development at UQ Business School, The University of Queensland, Brisbane, Australia.

Professor Härtel is recognized internationally as a leader in developing and translating new knowledge into management practices that foster human flourishing and the simultaneous achievement of personal and organizational aspirations. Her recent work in this area focuses on ethical leadership, sustainable change management practices, and developing and supporting resilience and well-being in the workplace. Her pioneering work on the characteristics of positive work environments has identified a number of individuals, groups, and organizational drivers of unhealthy and toxic work environments along with the leadership and human resource management strategies and practices to turn such situations around. Professor Härtel's work appears in over 60 book chapters and 100 refereed journal articles and she has won numerous awards internationally for her research. She is also the primary author of the wholly original textbook *Human Resource Management: Transforming Theory into Practice* (Pearson).

Dr. Amanda Roan is a senior lecturer in Human Resource Management, Employment Relations and Public Sector Management at the UQ Business School, University of Queensland, Brisbane, Australia. Her teaching spans the areas of human resource management and public sector management at both undergraduate and postgraduate levels and she has special interest and expertise in cross-cultural management education and internationalization of the curriculum. Her research is broadly focused on workforce participation with a special interest in gender and diversity at work. She has published in national and international journals, including *The Journal of Business Ethics* and *The Australian Journal of Political Science*. She has a long-standing successful record of supervising PhD students from a broad range of cultural backgrounds, including students from the Sultanate of Oman, Thailand, and Indonesia.

Introduction

In the quest to be recognized as critical to an organization's success as its profit-focused cousins, much of the language of contemporary Human Resource Management (HRM) textbooks mirrors the business-centered, bottom-line perspective. One need look no further than the discipline name to see this—people are not referred to as "people" but as "human resources." The current popularity of the word "talent" is also alarming when talents are divorced from the people who provide them. It is from this positioning that we introduce Giving Voice to Values (hereafter, GVV). The first author's approach to familiarizing students with the ethical issues in HRM and the features of ethical HRM practice are detailed in the remainder of this section. Following that, we share our collective thoughts on applying GVV to HRM practice and education along with some of the sample cases we use to provide students with the opportunity to develop their skills in giving voice to values.

Ethics in HRM

HRM is about people, and organizations are effective through people. An HRM practice that yields sustainable positive benefits therefore must be people-centered. For this reason, I like to begin my discussion of ethics in HRM with a slide titled, "Real Experiences of Real People Experiencing (un)ethical HRM in action." On the slide, I list some quotes obtained from interview studies I conducted with people in organizations that had recently downsized. These quotes, listed later in text, set the scene to get the students thinking about ethical issues in HRM, and importantly, that HRM needs to be people-centered (i.e., focusing on supporting the cognitive, emotional, and behavioral qualities of people to achieve outcomes good for both the business and its people) rather than narrowly business-centered (i.e., focusing on business outcomes and treating people simply as resources to get these done) in order to set the ethical context necessary for enduring positive outcomes for the organization.[1] This shift in thinking is akin to the shift in education from teacher-centered learning to student-centered learning.

- "I was just so traumatized at that time, seems silly now but at the time I was just traumatized, no, I never want to work for XYZ again"
- "The head of department... ended up in hospital with a heart problem after the redundancy meeting"
- "we didn't know it impacted so much on our health until we got sick"

- "I didn't feel too threatened right from the outset but other people did"
- "The people telling us the bad news were only doing their job... They were nearly crying too"
- "I don't actually blame them, I don't think they have the full story themselves"
- "(After I was sacked) most of them (my co-workers) were lovely... kissing me and hugging me so it was really nice"
- "(After I was sacked) people saw you coming down the hall and went back into their offices to avoid you, eyes down."

After sharing the aforementioned quotes and examples that students may wish to provide, I like to summarize the ethical context relating to HRM initiatives and interventions under the heading of "The Ethics of Changing Things." Here, I focus on two key points:

1. Failure to recognize and attend to emotions when designing and implementing change programs increases the likelihood of change failure, and
2. Change has personal consequences for people. These can be positive from the individual's perspective (e.g., greater flexibility, opportunity for growth, and improved work conditions) or negative (e.g., disrupted habits, loss of confidence, loss of face, loss of control, loss of workmates, loss of employment, loss of income, loss of status, and work intensification).

These two points illustrate that, both ethically and for business sustainability, HRM in organizations is obliged to think about the well-being of people in designing and implementing policies and practices. This means,

- providing opportunities for stakeholder input into planning instead of withholding information about the effect of the change on personal goals,
- providing appropriate support systems instead of leaving people to fend with the change for themselves,

- fostering a culture of emotional awareness and displaying interpersonal sensitivity in communication instead of avoiding the emotional discomfort that may come with open and quality communication, and

- monitoring emotional reactions in change stakeholder groups and honestly and openly examining the role of the change intervention or implementation in people's responses, instead of ignoring the emotional states of stakeholders of change or blaming the individual for resistance to change.

Recognizing these features of ethical organizational change practices, students are reminded of the stewardship role HRM plays in safeguarding a history of positive change efforts. Like any relationship, trust is earned, and when present, facilitates collaboration, creativity, and citizenship behaviors.[2] If trust is broken, however, a negative distrust spiral is set in motion, not only losing the benefits of trust, but provoking counterproductive work behaviors,[3] including unethical behavior or the failure to give voice to values.

To illustrate to the students how the workplace shapes what is possible for the people working in it, I use a short YouTube video clip that clearly and simply makes my point that, "Great Performances Do Not Occur in a Vacuum." The clip, found at http://www.youtube.com/watch?v=1fw1CcxCUgg, documents a high-school basketball team and the players' and fans' responses to the team's autistic assistant who dreamed of a chance to play in a game. After showing the clip, I ask the students to complete the following activity:

Reflecting on this clip and your own experiences, take 5 minutes to individually write down the characteristics of an environment that supports resilience and voice.

Following this activity, I ask the group to share their insights, collating these on the whiteboard. What emerges is the foundation for discussing the elements of a Positive Work Environment (PWE).[4]

Simply put, PWEs exist when people see their workplace as supporting human flourishing. The PWE concept is useful for setting the scene for GVV activities as it provides a clear framework for assessing the ethical implications of HRM plans, practices, and outcomes. More specifically, I put the case forward to students that *"The Fruits of Ethical HRM are Positive Work Environments (PWEs)."* Drawing on the evidence discussed by Härtel (2004; 2008) students are presented with seven summary characteristics of PWEs:

- Ensures a healthy and secure physical environment
- Recognizes the emotional aspects of work and supports employees to constructively manage
- Promotes inclusion (belongingness) and psychological safety
- Fosters constructive conflict and addresses destructive conflict
- Motivation through support not fear
- Just policies and decision making
- A diversity climate of openness, where strong organizational norms exist to view difference positively and as a source of learning and where diverse individuals' identity and affiliation needs are met
- Facilitates achievement of aspirations
- Leaders and co-workers are seen as trustworthy, fair, open to diversity, and encouraging.

To equip students to make ethical decisions and arguments relating to HRM practice, I provide them with evidence for not only the organizational benefits of PWEs, but also the enormous costs of negative work environments. Three areas I generally cover relate to bullying, discrimination, and the biological effects of stress. To illustrate the biological effects of stress, I like to show the diagram from the April 2012 issue of *Scientific American*,[5] which depicts how stress shuts down the higher order mental processes in the brain, leaving the primitive functions in charge. In my experience, students find this representation of brain functioning overwhelmingly convincing for the business benefits of avoiding a negative work environment.

Activities for Setting the Foundation for Ethical HRM Practice

Throughout the semester, and as part of defining ethical HRM practice, I have students consider the ethical implications of the topics we discuss. I do this in a large group discussion so that the students are exposed to a variety of perspectives on the topic, as will be the case in their organizational roles, and to ensure that the ethical issues relating to employment, work environment features, and change processes are well grasped. Additionally, essay questions such as the following are used as part of their assessment.

Essay Assignment Question 1:
Draw on the theories and research discussed in class and course readings to discuss the features of a talent management strategy that support employee engagement and a high performance culture. Include a discussion of ethical issues in your response.

Essay Assignment Question 2:
Your CEO recently announced that your organization is going to merge with one of your competitors. Since then there has been a lot of talk among the employees about how the organization will change. While some people seem to be excited about the possible changes that may occur, many appear to have become quite nervous and have been speculating about what the merger will mean for them. There is a lot of talk about departments being disbanded and a lot of employees appear to be quite worried about losing their jobs.
Question:
1. What are the ethical issues for HRM raised by this scenario?
2. Discuss how you would go about devising a change process strategy for this scenario that addresses these ethical issues?

The latter assignment provides students with an opportunity to not only practice identifying ethical issues, but also to design a change strategy that conforms with their values and those presented in the class as contributing to a PWE. Being skilled in both these aspects is an important foundation for ethical HRM practice as well as for applying the GVV approach.[6] In the next section, I describe how I have been recently using the GVV approach in the HRM classroom. The final case study provides an example where time and options are much more restricted.

Essay Assignment Question 3:
A manager in your organization recently came to you, the HR Director, raising concerns about the selection process followed in appointing the new director of her division. The manager indicated that she and a

number of the other managers in the division believed that the appointment did not reflect the best qualified candidate in the applicant pool, but rather nepotism. In addition, there is a lot of talk in the Division by employees about the appointment with many expressing concern about the future of the Division and some even disengaging from their work.

Question:
1. What are the ethical issues for HRM raised by this scenario?
2. Discuss how you would go about devising a strategy for this scenario that addresses these ethical issues?

Applying GVV to HRM

As the GVV technique has been discussed in detail elsewhere in this book, this chapter provides some of the guidelines we give students for applying GVV specifically to HRM, along with a sample of the GVV cases that we have included in our HRM curriculum.

When we introduce GVV to the classroom, we highlight when it is most likely to apply to HRM matters. Specifically, we point out that, in HRM, some ethical matters are covered by regulatory frameworks and when this is the case, such as for discrimination and harassment, action can be pursued through these means. Even when pursuing action through formal means, GVV offers the students a means of practicing difficult workplace conversations and interactions. GVV is, however, even more relevant where ethical matters are not covered by regulations or where individuals perceive that using formal channels poses a personal risk. Our discussion of GVV proceeds with this assumption.

After introducing the GVV technique to students, we identify its implications for the individual HRM practitioner as well as for the practice of HRM. In the case where an HRM practitioner recognizes an ethical issue where GVV is applicable, the individual can create a personal script. Although GVV allows students to chart their own approach to implementation, the emphasis on PWEs gives the class a clear direction for the desired outcome. After devising their course of action, the students embark on a personal plan. The personal plan contains a stakeholder analysis, identifying the key parties and what is at stake for them along with the rationalizations they are likely to use for their behavior. The stakeholder analysis reinforces the unique position occupied by HRM practitioners, that is, to serve the interest of the organization and the people within it. On the basis of this analysis, the practitioner develops a plan of what they will say and to whom to address the issue.

As many ethical issues in organizations are not directly observed by an HRM practitioner, ethical practice is dependent on the responses of a third party, or an observer, and can often involve complex situations. Ethical HRM demands that people work in an environment where they can give voice to values and that people have the skills to give voice to their values in a manner that optimizes an ethical outcome. The former is achieved through the ideas previously discussed regarding a positive work environment. The latter is achieved by putting into place mechanisms to train and support people in the use of GVV in the workplace. One of the dilemmas that observers of HRM issues face is deciding whether to give voice to values when the offended party asks for nothing to be done or when harm may be caused by speaking out. These situations often lead to preserving destructive cultures. Although many years of workplace coun-seling has encouraged the empowerment of those who find themselves victims to speak out, it also dictates that the individual who is giving voice to values may be doing so in the defense of another. It is this role that the responsible HRM practitioner may need to take. Performing stakeholder analysis as part of GVV is very important to avoid making things worse for the person the protagonist is trying to defend.

A challenge HRM practitioners are often confronted with is deter-mining where their loyalty lies, that is, choosing between what is right for the organization and what is good for the person. In putting GVV into practice, each individual has to decide how to meet their values effec-tively and thus HRM practitioners themselves may not always be under-taking the course of action that is most comfortable for them, but one that clearly supports their analysis of the situation. This means that the practitioner has to go beyond solving the dilemma to making a personal script for action. We deal with this challenge in the classroom by having group discussions of a topic first so that students can experience the range of perspectives people may have. An advantage of the GVV approach is that, although the preferred values-driven course of action is given in the GVV scenario, in a multicultural class room, there is the expectation that students can devise a personal course of action that suits their own strengths and situation. We then follow this by asking students to write a two-page personal script. Students are invited to share their scripts with backup examples on hand in the event that no volunteers emerge.

Besides asking students to generate their own examples of ethical HRM issues where GVV applies—we ask students to draw on recent media reports to do so—we also provide short cases for students to work on. Four such cases are provided below. The first two place the student in the role of the third party observer while the latter two place the student in the role of the HR manager.

The Case of Unequal Assignments

You are a new HR manager for a large commercial complex. You employ a group of security officers. You are anxious to review elements of their jobs to make these more rewarding for the security officers. While reviewing the job assignments, you notice that Mohammed, the only non-English-background security guard, is always assigned more outside patrols even in very cold weather. You also notice that he is always assigned outside duties across the most popular break times when the rest of the group stay inside and talk about football. When you ask the supervisor why this is the case, he tells you that Mohammed likes it this way and so do the others. You are now sure that this is discrimination as you have heard this supervisor being outspoken against recent refugees from the Middle East. You decide this needs examination.

Teaching Notes

As outlined previously, the students have been introduced to the concept of a PWE and its benefits for the individual and the organization. The students will also have been previously introduced to the role of the HRM manager and discussed the reality that serving both the interests of the company and the interests of the individual can lead to values conflict. "The Tale of Two Stories"[7] can be used to help students to understand speaking and acting on values through GVV if students have not already been introduced to this approach in this or other courses. Students should also be taken through an exercise of self-knowledge in which they might question their personal purpose, risk profile, communication style, loyalty profile, and self-image.[8] In this classroom they are HR managers, therefore it is useful to point out that they will be expected to deal with values conflict situations and thus self-examination becomes important so that they may assess their own fitness for this role. An understanding of purpose, risk profile, loyalty profile, and communication style can be very useful in the multicultural classroom as it reinforces to students the importance of individual differences and contexts in acting ethically. This allows students to raise issues about the cultural environment in which they will ultimately operate and to make the modifications they will need, without sacrificing their values.

The case of the unequal assignments can be used in a class dealing with diversity and or antidiscrimination. It is important to point out to students that no complaint has been made here. Many jurisdictions and organizations have mandated procedures for dealing with formal complaints. It is the HR manager's job to follow these through. The reality of an HR manager's life is that many complaints are informal, third party, or observed and thus the ability of giving voice becomes extremely important. Therefore the first question to students might be:

What values are being violated here? Why act?
This is an informal situation and they need to ask themselves what is at stake and for whom: the organization and its reputation, the organization's effort to create a PWE, and of course the actors and the HR manager. Students may also raise the legal obligation of an HR manager to make sure that discrimination doesn't occur in the organization. As pointed out in GVV[9] and as a fundamental of good HR practice, students should seek more information on the situation but should do so with care. Students are asked to examine the situation and to identify issues and key stakeholders. This brings up the question of approaching Mohammed and the appropriate communication strategies.

So what to do? First we usually advise students that they cannot transfer or dismiss the supervisor (which would allow them to avoid the issue). GVV emphasizes not only the importance of speaking up but also the importance of determining to whom you should speak and in what order.

This case requires the student to examine the question of who to speak to first. Likely responses include:

1. Approach Mohammed with his/her fears first.
2. Approach the supervisor with your concerns, making clear that this is your concern from an equity perspective.
3. Collect more information on implicit discrimination in the organization.

After this discussion, students are invited in groups to open the conversation depending on their chosen course of action. For example, a student who decides to talk with Mohammed first might come up with the following opening.

"Mohammed, I have noticed that you are working a lot of outside shifts. I am concerned that you are not being included in all aspects of the security section. What can we do about this?"

But Mohammed's response might be, "I am happy," and it is then up to students to find ways to keep the dialogue open, particularly as preliminary conversations with the supervisor have somewhat closed the conversation.

What else can be done? GVV also emphasizes the importance of identifying levers available to assist organizational managers to act ethically. Students can discuss how this situation sits with the whole idea of PWE and identify PWE supporters as allies. One of the levers open to students is the legal obligations to deal with discrimination. Students may decide to tackle the issue head on with the supervisor. An example of a script of HRM manager to supervisor might be:

"You are aware that we promote a positive work environment in this organization and we have a policy of embracing diversity. This means that people from all backgrounds must feel included and we need to develop their potential. I believe that Mohammed is being excluded. I want this to change. Let's discuss how we can bring this about."

A second lever may be HR interventions such as improving the job design of the security officers. Students who choose this option might like to tackle the situation by improving job design and empowering the security officers to have much more choice in the way they undertake and structure their assignments. This is not meant to imply that HR managers can avoid giving voice to values by this action, but rather this opens up an avenue for students to examine the raft of issues that may arise when they attempt change in an environment where this type of discrimination occurs. The teacher can challenge students by asking "how is the supervisor likely to respond to your initiative?" This can lead to identifying blockages and the rationalizations that they may encounter. Typically, these might include "Mohammed hasn't complained," "The supervisor is only joking," or "It's not really that bad." Depending on the class environment, (and some mischievous students are actually helpful here), students might identify the response of the supervisor as, "How dare you accuse me of being a racist?" or "I've tried but I don't know what to do." The scripts can be treated as "trees" with many branches with each branch having its blockages.

Regardless of the approach to values-driven action chosen by the students, this case highlights the complexity HR managers can face in dealing with discrimination cases. In addition, students leave this exercise equipped with a set of different possible scripts and action plans for voicing their values, as opposed to merely understanding how complex it may be.

The Case of Under-Rating

Sue has just returned to work from maternity leave. She has recently undertaken a performance review where she was rated using performance criteria and performance indicators that she could not have achieved given her absence from work. Her performance appraiser, who is much more senior than you, has been either careless in the delivery of the rating or used them inappropriately. You noticed that Sue had been visibly upset last week and you now think you understand why. How do you, as the HR manager, deal with this situation?

Teaching Notes

This case can be used within a class on performance appraisal methods. Typically, HRM classes teach the technical aspects of preparing performance appraisal instruments and the skills required in conducting a performance appraisal. They emphasize that performance appraisals should be valid, reliable, conducted in a constructive manner, and just and fair. Rarely are students instructed in what to do if an appraisal is not fair. As with the previous case, students should be prepared with the techniques of GVV. Discussion is likely to reveal that this is a clear case of an unfair appraisal, whether intentional or not. Whether maternity leave is an issue will be open to debate.

Students should be asked "What is at stake here for the key parties involved?" Having just been through a class or learning exercise that has emphasized the perception of integrity in performance appraisals as key to them being regarded as useful and valued by management and staff, students are likely to identify that this performance appraiser is undermining the integrity of the process and this can be damaging for the organization. This, as well as the denial of due process, should give the HR manager the impetus and responsibility to act. Of course, Sue is also a stakeholder as is the appraiser. Students might also identify the HR manager as a potential stakeholder, as this is a "managing upwards" context.

Given that they have a clear responsibility as the HR Manager to maintain the integrity of the appraisal system, students are most likely to write a script that is "armed" with the technical aspects of performance appraisal. Examples of these levers may include:

"Sue has just returned from maternity leave therefore this appraisal is inappropriate." They might like to add, "I need to make you aware that we have obligations under anti-discrimination provisions to make sure that maternity leave is taken into account."

Again, these scenarios can be extended by "branching." The exercise could end with an agreement, or it can be extended to deal with a defiant rater (who has a higher position in the organization hierarchy to you), or it can be extended to planning a culture change in regard to gender equity at work. Students should also be asked, "How are you going to deal with Sue and the damage that may have been caused to her confidence and self-esteem"?

As, in HR terms, this basically comes down to performance management, this becomes an HR skills building exercise as well as one in giving voice to values.

The Case of Looking the Other Way

You recently joined an organization as one of its HR officers. You were asked to serve as the HR representative on the selection committee for a new executive appointment. Three internal candidates were interviewed for the position, only one of whom has extensive management experience. The Vice President (VP) to whom the new appointment would report wanted to select a less experienced candidate. Considerable debate occurred before the decision was taken to appoint the VP's preferred candidate. Later you learned that the new appointment was a friend of the VP's family, and that they regularly socialized outside work. You shared your concern that nepotism had played a role in the appointment with your HR Director but were told that this is how things are done around here. You think that this compromises the integrity of the HR Department.

Teaching Notes

This case deals with entrenched unethical behavior within a company or organizational silence, and issues that are "off the radar" of consideration. The context here is that a powerful VP gets what he/she wants in this company regardless of the ethics involved. Although the new HR manager may easily recognize the wrongdoing, others have come to live with it and accept it.

It is likely that students will find the idea that giving voice in this situation is an overwhelming prospect. It is unlikely that students are going to decide to challenge the VP. This case can open up a discussion on ethical climate. If unethical behavior is tolerated in selection processes it is likely that it occurs throughout the organization. Links between ethical climate and PWE can be explored through this discussion. At this point some students may indicate that they would not want to work for such an organization. GVV offers an avenue to give students a deeper understanding of situations where unethical behavior has become normalized. Gentile stresses that acquiring the ability to give voice to values can be a developmental process.[10] The story of Lisa Baxter in Gentile's work illustrates how thoughtful responses, refusing to respond to unethical requests, and actions can bring about change.[11]

GVV provides a set of assumptions, or thought experiments, to create a "safe enabling space" for experimentation and creativity in voicing values. Students can be asked the question:

How can you create a "safe enabling space" in which to voice values and influence change?

The three following assumptions can be used to guide the discussion.[12]

Assumption: I have voiced my values, at some point in my past
The teacher can point out that the new HR officer has already given voice about her concerns to the HR manager and that, although he/she got an unsatisfactory response, nothing terrible happened. Indeed, a dialogue already has opened up with the HR manager. Students can now consider options for further dialogue.

Assumption: It is easier for me to voice my values in some contexts than others
Following on from the previous assumption, students can explore the HR department as a safe space to give voice to values. Recruitment and selection may not be the only HR procedures where unethical behavior is exhibited. Using learning from other discussion in the HR class, students can explore ways in which they may express concerns beyond this one incident. There are a number of possible approaches that may be devised by the students. Four examples are summarized here:

(a) Earlier discussions of the role of HR professionals will have introduced the idea of the HR officer as an internal consultant. That is, line managers perform the HR function and the HR office is called in to give advice. Here students should feel legitimately able to give this advice, which includes advice on HR integrity and best practice. This advice may not be followed but it will become part of the conversation within the organization.

(b) The second HR function that students are likely to identify lies within the training and development function. It is good HR practice to provide basic training for those involved in HR functions such as recruitment and selection, performance management, promotion, and exit. This can include the writing of policy, presentations, and the writing of practice manuals. The production of these with the inclusion of values can be encouraged.

(c) Depending on the jurisdiction, students are also likely to raise "fear of litigation" as an enabling context. This can be explored in relation to (a) and (b).

(d) In the context of this class, the pursuit of and the advantages of a PWE are likely to be raised.

Assumption: I am not alone

This case highlights that unethical behavior can become normalized in an organization. Normalization does not necessarily mean a lack of awareness.[13] Students can explore the likelihood of others feeling uncomfortable with the situations they encounter, how such persons can be identified, and what can be learnt from the experience of their peers. In this case we are talking about a reasonably large organization where there are more than one HR officer. Students can be asked the question:

"How are you going to be able to identify allies?"

Likely avenues for the identification of allies by students include:

(a) Others in the HR department.

(b) The staff who act on selection and promotion panels.

(c) Listening and paying attention to conversations where people express their frustration with current practice, and as GVV points out, collecting critically important information.

It is important here to emphasize the value of students preparing scripts for their questions and for dealing with likely responses. This can include the rationalization already encountered in the case study—that is just the way things are done around here. Simple examples of students' responses to this rationalization may include, "Are you happy with this?" "I find this difficult to reconcile with what we are trying to do here," "Can you suggest some ways forward?"

Rather than simply being a short exercise within a class on recruitment and selection, this exercise can take many directions and result in multiple courses of actions and a broad variety of scripts. Here we add a note of caution to those working within a multicultural classroom. In some cultures, favoring family and friends might be considered a duty. This does not mean the exercise is not useful. It can become an interesting scenario for exploring giving voice to values in the multinational firm.

The Case of Downsizing Without Due Process

You work as an HR Officer in a government office whose staffing budget has been cut by 20 percent. Without consultation with the HR department, you have been told that employees on fixed-term contracts rather than permanent positions will be the first targets for dismissal and that many of these positions are to be terminated and paid out immediately. You then were given a list of the most expendable positions by the HR manager. You have been told to prepare an e-mail that will be sent to the staff who will be losing their jobs at the end of the week. Although you have no power to reverse the decision over whom and how many staff will lose their jobs the process really worries you.

Teaching Notes

In many public service environments around the world, this has been a frequent event in recent years. Financial crisis and political expediency have meant that downsizing has often been hard and fast despite many years of research showing that a poorly conducted downsizing exercise can have a lasting negative impact on individuals and organizations. In Master's level classes where some students might have had an experience such as outlined in this case, these students will often express cynicism that a PWE is even possible. In contrast to the previous case, there is very little time to act here. As with the other cases, students are required to analyze the situation and undertake a stakeholder analysis. Students need to examine what is at stake for the employees who are losing their jobs, employees who survive the downsizing, the management, the organization, and the HR manager. Putting themselves into the shoes of the HR manager writing the e-mail is likely to bring about an emotive response and it is useful to draw on self-examination exercises here. Students should be encouraged to examine the situation carefully. It is likely that students will come to the realization that a 20 percent cut will mean that their own jobs might be at risk. This can lead to an examination of rationalizations such as, "I am a public servant therefore I must obey this directive"; "this is going to hurt people anyway, so what does it matter how this is done"; "I need to keep my own job"; or "I am probably next."

GVV emphasizes that there will be a range of personal responses in any situation. Gentile states that the driving force behind a person's decision to give voice to values can be "their identity as a cautious or even fearful person, while others think that it is their identity as risk taker and bold leader."[14] As shall be shown subsequently, the range of responses can produce a number of rationalizations among the students and a lively discussion of risk taking and its consequences. The possible responses include:

(a) It is possible that some students will say that there is nothing they can do and their solution may be to write an e-mail in the most humane way they can. This could include a justification that "I need to protect my own job." These students can be encouraged to examine how this e-mail can be written.

(b) Our experience of the multicultural classroom also shows that "obedience to authority" weighs heavier in some cultures than in others. This does not mean that these students don't wish to express their values. Reframing of choices can be helpful here (see following text). These students can be encouraged to examine how a solution can be reached with deference to authority and/or with the approach of maintaining harmony.

(c) Other students might take a stand and refuse to write the e-mail. An interesting student response might be a rationalization such as, "Well I am probably going to lose my job in a couple of months— I'll go down fighting." Students can be asked to examine the implications of this stance and what it achieves as a solution.

(d) In a class that has emphasized a PWE, and when dealing with the topic of workplace change and HRM process, students are likely to be prepared to argue that downsizing needs to be conducted in a way that preserves people's dignity. Further, the HRM and organizational behavior literature provides numerous examples of the impact of badly conducted downsizing exercises. It is clear that in this situation, although the HR department cannot reverse the decision, they may be able to influence the process. The solutions students generate are likely to be similar to the other cases but here speed is an imperative. Identifying allies and audiences remains important. A list of allies is likely to include the HR manager and line managers who will find this course of action unethical and unproductive.

Importantly, response (b) and (d) open up "change the frame" as forming part of the solution. That is, speaking up in this case is not being disloyal to the HR manager or, in the public sector context, acting in accordance with government policy as directed, but acting for the good of the organization. In this case, this means using good HR process to mitigate the impact on the work unit and individuals. Students can be encouraged to develop a change management plan within the context of a script that they must present to their HR manager. This usually means a face-to-face interview informing the staff member of the decision, a dignified exiting process, and outplacement support. Remind the students frequently that they only have a short time to act.

Conclusion

Although rarely stated explicitly, HRM practice that yields sustainable positive benefits is necessarily ethical. Understanding the ethical dimensions of HRM strategy and practices is the first step in being able to engage in ethical HRM and to give voice to values on HRM matters.

Three key ethical dimensions that students of HRM need to be aware of are the role of work in society, the role the work environment plays in human experience, and how people respond to change. First, it is essential for students to recognize that work is the vehicle that provides people with the opportunity for economic participation. Accessing and retaining work and improving employment status therefore represent the quality of life an individual can have and give their loved ones. Ethical HRM minimizes barriers to access, recognizes the potential power imbalance between employee and employer and thus the opportunity for exploitation, and takes steps to ensure fairness of decision making relating to employment opportunities.

Second, students need to recognize that the experiences individuals are exposed to at work can empower and enhance flourishing *or* disempower and create psychosocial harm. Ethical HRM takes accountability for the work environment, ensuring bullying does not occur and that there is a diversity open climate. Third, students need to be mindful of the personal consequences change has for people. Ignoring these or failing to minimize the negative impact of change initiatives puts people at risk (e.g., loss of confidence, loss of face, loss of control, loss of workmates, loss of employment, loss of income, loss of status, and work intensification). Ethical HRM supports people's resilience and interpersonal sensitivity. *Good intentions are not enough.* Ethical HRM understands how humans respond to change and the things that help or hurt their adaptation. It actively works to ensure the well-being of both the organization and its people.

Sustainable HRM practices require a keen awareness of the ethical implications associated with the multiflorous dimensions of managing people. This includes system-level issues, managerial-level issues, and individual employee-level issues. In this chapter, we described some of the key ethical issues associated with the practice of HRM, some key features of ethical practice (i.e., ethical design and implementation and ethical work environments) and shared some of the ways in which we have integrated the GVV approach into our HRM curriculum. The sample activities we included have been effectively used at the undergraduate and Master's level as well as in Executive Education.

One of the key challenges organizations face is promoting a high performance workplace while avoiding the toxicity that can readily develop when competiveness gets out of hand. When people perceive they are not valued, are unfairly treated, or unsupported, they are likely to engage in counterproductive work behaviors (e.g., negative word of mouth about the organization, angry outbursts, bullying, absenteeism, presenteeism, and theft). A positive work environment, which promotes human well-being and ethicality, is the antidote. Promoting a PWE, however, requires that people give voice to values regarding activities that are absent but required for a PWE as well as activities that are present, which pose a threat to a PWE. For HRM managers, this means that they need to be equipped to challenge HRM policies and practices that are undermining to a PWE as well as to advocate for those policies and practices that underpin a PWE. It also means that they need to be equipped with techniques for empowering the workforce so that all staff have the tools and incentive to actively work in the interests of a PWE. GVV is an important tool in the HRM manager's toolkit for achieving these aims as it gives students a way to rehearse actions that will help promote the actual existence of PWEs.

CHAPTER 6

Giving Voice to Values for the Public Sector

An Exploratory Approach

Kenneth Wiltshire
and Stephen Jones

Abstract

This chapter affirms the relevance and significant benefits of using the GVV approach in education and professional development relating to the public sector. However, it is argued that, while there are many similarities in the functioning of the private and public sectors, there are fundamental and unique aspects of the public sector that need to be acknowledged in the curriculum development pertaining to this sector. These relate mainly to the "Political" context (i.e., the politics of the system of government), and its associated accountability framework, which is often complex. A broad exploratory approach to GVV curriculum development is offered, on the basis of the experience at the University of Queensland Business School, in an endeavor to generate more discussion (and cases) by academics and public sector officials.

Keywords

values, public sector, accountability, appeal processes.

Author Biography

Dr. Stephen Jones is lecturer in Public Sector Management at The University of Queensland Business School. He formerly served in a policy capacity in local and state governments in Queensland and Western Australia as well as academic positions in Victoria. His research interests focus on examination of comparative policy measures by local governments in both Australian and international contexts and the role of local government managing the development of cities and urban environments and focus on encouraging innovation and creativity to reduce the impact of climate change. He has published in international and Australian journals as well as completed comprehensive reports on regional development in Queensland. He is also an associate Research Fellow at the Institute for Public Policy at Curtin University and an associate with the center for local government at the University of New England.

Professor Kenneth Wiltshire is the J.D. Story Professor of Public Administration at The University of Queensland Business School. He has served as a consultant and an adviser to prime ministers and premiers, royal commissions, government departments, government business enterprises, and the private sector. For 9 years, he served as a member of the Commonwealth Grants Commission, was consultant to the Australian Advisory Council on Intergovernmental Relations, was a founding board member of the Constitutional Centenary Foundation, and was a member of the Inquiry into the Brisbane City Council and Australian Metropolitan Governance in the 1980s. Professor Wiltshire served for 6 years as Australia's Representative on the Executive Board of UNESCO and was the inaugural chair of the Wet Tropics World Heritage Management Committee. He is a national fellow of the Institute of Public Administration Australia and is an honorary trustee of CEDA and a member of its national research council. He was awarded the Order of Australia in 1998 for services to policy making, public administration, and UNESCO.

Introduction

At first glance, it might seem that employees in the public sector who are faced with moral and ethical dilemmas over perceived or experienced actions have a significant variety of opportunities to have their grievances and fears addressed. This is probably true for all countries, since even repressive regimes tend to display an array of appeal and investigative mechanisms surrounding their public sectors. Of course, if a whole nation is imbued with a culture of corruption the public sector will not be immune; indeed, it may be the gene pool. No matter how elaborate and impressive sounding the institutional structure of investigative mechanisms may be, the corrupt cultural influence will be all-pervasive and render the institutional framework rotten.

In democratic nations, with a stable regime of the rule of law, universal standard freedoms and rights, a healthy separation of powers, and a free press, it is generally the case that the public sector will contain a barrage of bodies, unknown in the private sector, all charged with maintaining the accountability of official behavior. Public servants working in these systems can be exposed to situations that challenge their personal values. The unique feature of the public sector is the political dimension that underpins the tasks and responsibilities of the officials. Many are attracted to work in public sector agencies on the basis of the service they can provide leading to improvements in their communities. Much of the work performed involves questions of the public good it will provide. Of course, public servants recognize the fact that they need to work in conjunction with political representatives and there are situations when their personal values face challenges from more overtly political objectives that bring opportunities for ethical dilemmas to emerge. It is this dimension that marks one of the most significant differences between the challenges faced by those working in the public sector and those in the private sector. For senior managers, the political issues involved in their dealings with political representatives can sometimes lead to conflict. The bodies charged with ensuring accountability provide formal mechanisms to deal with such situations and civil servants are open to pursue them to help ensure their concerns can be voiced. Some are external to the executive branch; others are internal. Consider this checklist of the various branches in the system of governance based on the separation of powers, taking Westminster models as a case study.

Legislative Branch

Parliament and its many committees are the focal point of responsible government in Westminster systems. Although public servants are meant to have their dealings with politicians through their Chief Executive and Minister, there are many occasions when they meet the elected members face to face and have the opportunity to develop personal connections with them. In more enlightened regimes, the government permits public servants to be examined by parliamentary committees without the need for the minister to act as an intercessory. Public Accounts Committees and Estimates Committees are key examples where the financial probity of the government is under the telescope and microscope and the public servants are in the cross hairs. Formal and informal opportunities are therefore presented to them to report corruption and malfeasance in the executive branch openly or by a nod and a wink. The same is true in relation to other parliamentary committees charged with oversight of the government's legal, personnel, and physical functioning. Subtle wording, often in code, in the department's annual report to parliament can also be a springboard.

There have indeed been many instances where public servants have been able to use this interface to reveal and pursue behavior that they believed to be improper. But it is a hazardous pathway involving complete trust in politicians and their capacity to pursue a matter effectively and without primary regard for seeking political advantage. Any consequent embarrassment to the government of the day risks severe retribution. Moreover, it strikes at the traditional and accepted hierarchical line of accountability since it is the Minister who must accept ultimate responsibility for misdemeanours despite the attempt in some jurisdictions to delegate legal responsibility to Agency Heads as Accountable Officers. In Australia, this issue has long historical roots as revealed in a famous case where a government agency head leaked information about what he believed to be corrupt behavior by his minister and, despite his accusations being found to be correct, he was summoned before the Bar of Parliament to defend himself. His statement rings out across the decades:

> I have never wavered in the opinion that an officer in my position … has a higher duty to the people of the State than to his Minister or any member of the government of the day and that he is justified in taking the most effective means available to serve that duty.[1]

Parliament voted on party lines to dismiss him.

In a republican system of government with a more distinct separation of powers, such as the United States, the Congress may well have more independence and firepower to follow-up trails laid by concerned public servants, but the potential for retribution is no less.

Of course, there are also a number of para-parliamentary bodies tasked with overseeing day-to-day behavior of public servants, and who offer a reporting haven of sorts for disaffected officials. The Auditor-General is the oldest of these institutions, and the past 50 years or so have witnessed the creation of further bodies such as Ombudsmen, Integrity Commissioners, and Information Commissioners administering Freedom of Information legislation. They all tend to be technically Officers of Parliament and not government. They generally have a sound record of independence in the pursuit of their clear mandates and have weeded out much corrupt and bad behavior following complaints from public servants. However, their checks are nowadays random and selective since their budgets do not permit the old-fashioned comprehensive fiduciary and compliance oversight. Their pace has slowed exponentially as they are grossly under-resourced for the potential number of cases they face. Moreover, in most Westminster systems, the executive and not the parliament decides their budget and staffing levels because most speakers of parliaments have "wimped out" in standing up for these and all other members of the parliamentary family on resourcing decisions including for the parliament itself. A public servant with a complaint to make can no longer be completely assured that the complaint will be taken up. Moreover, these oversight bodies have taken to working with the agencies concerned in investigating complaints against them, sometimes even delegating the complaint to the agency itself to address. This hardly inspires confidence in potential complainants and certainly blows their cover.

Judicial Branch

A somewhat similar picture emerges from examination of the workings of the judicial branch. Courts are effective (if somewhat slow and expensive) in addressing illegal behavior, and there is a solid body of Administrative Law in place in most jurisdictions. But much of the behavior, suspected or experienced by aggrieved public servants, may rest on hearsay evidence or be related to actions that are immoral or unethical in nature, rather than being strictly illegal. Moreover, there is limited confidentiality in a court hearing. Going to court is a daunting prospect, especially given its adversarial nature.

To address the inappropriateness of the courts in these circumstances, in a similar vein to the para-parliamentary scene, the past 50 years or so have seen the addition of a range of para-judicial institutions. The list includes bodies such as Crime Commissions, Anti-Corruption Commissions, and various generalist or specialist appeal tribunals. Although possessing legal powers, their operations tend to be less adjudicatory, less adversarial, and often less formal. Some do work in conjunction with police and other law enforcement bodies where clear legal breaches may also be involved. However, these bodies like their para-parliamentary cousins, suffer the same resource deprivation at the hands of the executive branch, take up only a proportion of all the cases referred to them, and sometimes delegate the investigation back to the agency where the alleged offence is claimed to have occurred. From a complainant's point of view, a worst-case scenario occurs when the police are seconded to these bodies and then are engaged in investigating police behavior. This is not a good look, yet the practice is becoming more familiar. The situation is compounded if the police service has its own internal ethics enforcement unit and the external crime commission defers to that internal process.

The Regulatory Branch

As governments around the world in recent times have pursued privatization, corporatization, outsourcing, and partnerships, a large proportion of public bodies have become subject to the same economic pressures faced by the private sector, whereas previously they were shielded. This is especially so where economic activity is occurring and notably in infrastructure or service provision. This space of government–business relations is a fertile arena for corruption of various kinds and many public servants have been caught with their hands in the till or their pockets lined with offerings from grateful clients. But the regulatory field also opens up a two-way process whence public servants themselves may report instances of corruption by their masters or colleagues. Regulators tend to offer somewhat more confidentiality than other avenues of appeal and so may be more attractive to an aggrieved potential complainant. This is probably more the case in countries such as Australia where regulation is seen as a preventive instrument, unlike the United States where a different culture seems to prevail with regulators seen as antifree enterprise, and whose main role appears to be one of closing the stable door after the horse has bolted.

However, once again, in this field we come up against resource constraints for the regulators. This is often compounded by significant risks to their budgets should they launch unsuccessful litigation. Very few regulators take up all the complaints lodged with them and any "own source" initiatives are carefully appraised before being launched. It is also often a very time-consuming process and hence a harrowing one for a complainant.

The field of regulation also encompasses an international dimension. Nations that have ratified international conventions take on added obligations to adhere to universal norms and standards, many of which relate to ethical and accountable conduct on the part of public officials. This is most evident in the several human rights and freedoms instruments of the United Nations, and also in many of those of the International Labour Organisation. There are also relevant instruments relating to trade and investment, banking, aviation, migration, and so on. An aggrieved public servant with concerns in these areas might well take a complaint to the international bodies that oversee these instruments, and many have done so. The stakes are high here since a complainant runs the risk of being labeled unpatriotic or worse, and their identity cannot be guaranteed to remain confidential since subsequent investigations will attract high-profile media coverage. This is true even if the complaint is made via a domestic peak organization, such as trade union or environmental or human rights organization or an NGO. It is also often a necessarily slow drawn-out process.

Inside the Executive Branch

Needless to say, most modern public services also have their own internal elaborate network of accountability mechanisms. Mostly, they are formulated in an enforceable Code of Conduct or set of Organizational Principles and Practices. These usually include designated complaints processes for a spectrum of misbehaviors from bribery and corruption to discrimination, bullying, patronage, favoritism, misappropriation, and unethical conduct however defined. All of these mechanisms tend to come under the jurisdiction of a central personnel agency charged with the general Human Resource Management function for the public sector.

In recent times, following the well-worn adage of "Let the Managers Manage," governments have weakened the powers of these central personnel agencies forcing them to delegate the operation of this appeal and investigative processes to departmental agency heads. The central agency is then relegated to merely standard setting, oversight, and training roles, thus opening the way for uneven application and rigor across the service. The weakening of the powers of these central agencies, usually known as public service commissions, has also been part of the perceptible trend toward politicization of the public service in Westminster systems. When public service commissions served as a buffer between ministers and public servants politicization was less likely to occur. All this has been exacerbated by other changes in the trappings of the senior levels of the public service, including placing public servants on fixed-term contracts, and making the oversight and renewal of those contracts subject to the whim of the head of government. Add to this the emerging murky modern role of staff in ministerial offices and the result is a blurring of the whole political/administrative interface. In such circumstances, a public servant is far less likely to have confidence and trust in the possibility of receiving impartial nonpolitical consideration of any grievance or complaint from the head of the department.

The Plight of the Whistle-Blower

It was precisely to address the dilemmas facing potential aggrieved complainants from both within or outside the public service that many nations have introduced whistle-blower protection legislation. Sometimes the whistle-blowing provisions are handled by an external para-judicial body; sometimes by an internal public sector agency. The results are very discouraging. Various studies show that the whistleblowers are rarely able to keep their identities secret if they wish to do so. Moreover, the vast majority have suffered severely either medically, or in their career prospects, and generally both. Despite their accusations often being vindicated, they are usually ostracized by their colleagues and their communities.[2]

The Missing Dimension

So it can be seen that the public sector contains a labyrinth of accountability and reporting mechanisms. When CEOs who have served in both the private and public sectors are asked to identify the main differences they encountered in the public sector, the first words they tend to utter are "complexity and interference," usually spoken in a bitter tone. Yet, for all the elaborate grievance pathways in the public sector, it still tends to fail in giving confidence to employees to take action and speak out about improper behavior.

Some of the reasons for this are systemic. We have seen how most of these appeal avenues are resource constrained, not comprehensive in their processes, and so unable to guarantee a full investigation. Many are not truly independent of government; indeed, the leaders of all these bodies are often appointed through a heavy government influence and their budgets are government controlled. Some are vulnerable to politicization, and the modern public servant cannot even be totally sure of receiving a nonpolitical hearing from his or her Departmental Head. These are structural deficiencies that are not likely to change in the short term, if at all; despite the constant often mindless restructuring that typifies government bureaucracies in the modern age. Recently introduced "state of the service" reports in several developed countries have revealed a widespread lack of confidence on the part of public servants in the leadership of their organizations and inadequate attention to the morale and welfare of employees—indeed, HRM practices in general leave a lot to be desired.[3]

It also needs to be recognized that the public sector milieu differs from that of the private sector in important respects. It is true that the nature of complaints is often similar, for example, discrimination, corruption, bribery, collusion, bullying, favoritism, unethical conduct, and so on. A major Australian seminar and case study workshop, conducted by the University of Queensland Business School (UQBS), recently discovered that a considerable proportion was simply the result of bad HRM practices, as also happens frequently in the private sector. The differences are generally to be found in the context and motivation surrounding the alleged offences. Political factors will be very much to the fore and permeate the mind of the potential complainant as he or she contemplates what action they will take, and decides through which of the myriad appeal avenues open to them they will venture with their concerns. It is also the case that public sector malfeasance, particularly when senior managers and chief executives are involved, will face considerably more probing and potential exposure from the media, and so the identity of the complainant or whistle-blower will be far more likely to be revealed and analyzed. Political masters will often quickly disclaim responsibility and even seek to cast doubt on the motivation and character of the complainant. In short, in a public sector context, facing up to making a complaint is an extremely daunting and stressful experience. It is the fears associated with the consequences of these actions that serve as the most common reasons and rationalizations preventing public servants from acting on their values and raising their voice. It is in this context that the promise of the Giving Voice to Values (GVV) approach provides its most powerful message. The "post-decision-making" approach to ethical dilemmas provides public servants with a vehicle to voice their values by providing the tools with how to respond considering their best interests and achieving the most effective outcome. It is clear that the solution to the achievement of a public sector with high morale, confidence, and integrity will lie in the behavioral realm and not the structural one. The incorporation of GVV into the toolkit of public servants will be an important element for current and future senior managers and general staff as public sector agencies deal with the challenges of the modern world. The UQBS has been an early adopter of GVV into its curriculum for both public and private sector management students. The approach has been the subject of 2 years of pilot studies at UQBS in the Public Sector Management major of the Master of Business degree.

Clearly, the focus of GVV is exactly what is required to give public sector employees the awareness and skills to navigate the appeal channels and tunnels at their disposal. This approach can be introduced into academic studies that current and aspiring public sector employees undertake. The preferred approach in the postgraduate Public Sector Management courses at UQBS has been the *Functional* or *Topical Model* as described in the GVV curriculum guide. It is important to recognize the diversity of occupations within public sector agencies with each having their own specializations and professional requirements. Students at the UQBS courses are provided with insights into the contemporary issues faced by the modern public sector. Discussions around some of the ethical dilemmas that can emerge provide the perfect opportunity for GVV to be used as the leading approach for individuals to manage their personal and professional integrity in the face of pressures they may encounter.

GVV can also be introduced into the formal professional development and training programs of the public sector itself. This approach has been initiated with the recent major seminar and a UQBS GVV case writer's workshop held in partnership with the Queensland Government's Public Sector Management Commission and in association with the Institute of Public Administration Australia. One of the key outcomes of the workshop has been the development of a series of case studies that can serve as the basis for group discussions and individual assignments associated with the application of GVV in UQBS courses. These case studies will begin to form an integral component of the contribution that GVV can make to the preparation of students to learn the techniques of overcoming their rationalizations for not giving voice to their values. Most importantly, these cases emerge from real-world experience of public servants when performing their responsibilities in public sector settings. Through the analysis of GVV case studies, students learn to recognize reasons and rationalizations that discourage voice, consider what is at stake for the major parties, and develop a powerful and persuasive response to the rationalizations against speaking up. An example of a case study is outlined as follows.

Case Study—Giving Voice to Values

Theme: Inappropriate use of resources.
Skills that can be used in the solution:

- managing up
- honest reporting

Barriers to taking action: Terry is a new recruit into a project team in a government agency where the culture was heavily affected by the presence of several strong personalities in senior positions. Speaking against the collective wishes was known to be a career-limiting move, and likely in the short term to result in exclusion from the group.

Case for students: Terry is a member of a project team responsible for constructing a large, government-funded medical facility. Completing the contract had provided a great deal of prestige to Terry's government agency that had won the job in a competitive tendering process against private sector operators. Several people on the project team expected their participation in the project to help them achieve their career ambitions. The project team was top-heavy, with many senior members providing strategic inputs and few "worker bees" actually doing the work. The project was part of a large federal government program that had clear objectives and stringent reporting requirements. Owing to the contract having a high public profile, politicians were always showing a great deal of interest and, as a consequence, their micro-management often led to changes to the way the project was implemented. Although appointed as a "worker bee," Terry ensured that she properly understood the program objectives, and her team's role in executing the contract appropriately in order to meet the requirements of the tender, which was now a public document.

During one of the project team meetings, Terry was directed to purchase expensive office furniture for the medical facility. When she raised concern about the purchase not being in accordance with the program objectives and about its considerable impact on the relevant line item of the budget, she was firmly told that the purchase was to be made and no further discussion was required.

Following this meeting, Terry reviewed the contract and the program objectives and consulted the project solicitor to ensure she understood the terms and conditions correctly. Terry remained concerned that purchasing the expensive office furniture breached the terms of the contract with the federal government and amounted to what she believed was an unnecessary waste of public funds. She prepared the information for the next team meeting, highlighting the specific areas of concern in the contract and providing an alternative course of action. This information and accompanying recommendation were poorly received at the meeting, with Terry's superiors advising that she did not understand the contract as they did.

How does Terry ensure her values are voiced?

Case studies based on public sector examples help to raise the issues specific to the sector. While there will be similarities in all organizational settings, there are elements within the public sector that are somewhat unique. One of the distinguishing features is the emphasis on the process and the need to abide by specific procedures that help guarantee transparency in decision making. There is often an underlying concern that some elements of the process will raise issues that can be exposed in the media and lead to political embarrassment for the minister and the government. Specifically, aggrieved citizens or businesses can voice their concerns and protests to the media thereby risking the smooth running of projects and programs. Another concern within a political context is the rationale for decisions. There has been desire within both academia and public sector agencies to base decisions on the use of evidence. In many instances, however, decisions can be based on political opportunity for the government, which can be concerning for many public servants and contribute to a clash of values. The case study above has been used to raise these issues for students.

The case has been used in public sector management courses at UQBS when discussing concepts and notions such as transparency, accountability, and political interference. The objective of the exercise is to identify reasons and rationalizations, key stakeholders, and implications of Terry failing to raise her concerns. Students are asked to examine the case study prior to coming to class and consider their response to the question. In the class, students are asked to discuss the issues in small groups of three to five and outline how they would individually respond to the issues. To help reinforce the issues being discussed, students are also required to identify and consider a time when they faced a value conflict at work, apply the GVV principles and consider how they could have responded more effectively. Students have already read and discussed the "Tale of

Two Stories" case study in earlier classes so they are familiar with the basic concepts of GVV. Part of the group exercise that works well has been the opportunity to role-play with scripts prepared by students prior to the class. Students are given the opportunity to voice the values in front of their peers in a way they think Terry might respond to her superiors. In our initial trials, students tended to react using the well-known response of focusing on the existing appeal avenues and taking their grievance to one of these channels. This is because, as we have outlined, the public sector has a plethora of such bodies. Hence, the introduction of GVV approaches is probably more challenging than for the private sector. Instructors have encouraged students to examine the GVV Module on *Scripts and Skills Readings* to develop initiatives such as "scripting" a possible response that would include consideration of the *Action Framework* and its "to do list" approach to developing a response that can best represent the values of the individual student. Public sector students certainly respond well to the notion of an action plan utilizing these scripts as this forms part of a process-based approach familiar to the public service. Of course, there is a benefit from considering the techniques successfully applied in other contexts and the Lockheed Martin *Voicing Our Values Techniques* has proven to be a valuable tool in this regard.

An Exploratory Framework

On the basis of their experience, academics at UQBS suggest it is now possible to outline an exploratory curriculum framework that could form the essence of a GVV program designed specifically for public sector employees.

1. *Values*: As in all curriculum development , the starting point must be the fundamental values that will underpin the curriculum. These should contain the personal values associated with all sound organizations including honesty, integrity, fairness, and respect. But the value framework in this case also needs to include many of the traditional values associated with the public sector itself, including public interest (as opposed to sectional or private interest), not just client but also citizen orientation, equity efficiency and effectiveness, trust

continuity and stability, compassion, and political neutrality with no discrimination.

2. *Motivation*: In the first instance, it is necessary to revisit the motivation for working in a public sector, which seems to have been lost after more than a decade of conflicting messages coming from cutbacks, managerial philosophies, and loss of faith by the public in politicians and hence the whole system of governance. This discussion links directly to one of the GVV Seven Pillars: Purpose. Clearly, there are tensions here that need to be brought out into the open and explored. The traditional view was that serving the public interest primarily motivated public servants. They also received the buzz of being close to the policy action, be able to improve the lives of citizens, and be quick to identify the need for modifications in policy implementation through service delivery. Their permanent tenure gave them security to provide frank and fearless advice to their political masters and enabled career planning. All this compensated for the somewhat lower remuneration they would receive as they climbed the hierarchy in comparison with the private sector financial rewards.

3. *Context*: Public servants will need some assurance that instructors and their curriculum content take cognizance of the unique features of the public sector context or else they will not have confidence in the whole exercise. This means, fundamentally, a recognition that the public sector is different from the private sector in some important respects. As outlined earlier, these revolve around the political milieu, the accountability regimes, the sheer complexity of reporting arrangements, the interagency relationships, and the goldfish-bowl work environment. It also extends to the incentive and remuneration framework of the public sector that is far more rigid, more risk averse, less responsive, and overall less generous than in the private sector.

4. *Distinguishing from HRM*: As mentioned, our experience in GVV case writing workshops with public sector officials has revealed that many of the issues that have arisen have their roots in bad human resource management practices rather than basic conflicts of values or ethics or corrupt behavior. To the extent that it is possible, any faults or missing dimensions in HRM policies and practices need to be identified early on to allow the instruction to focus on the key

element of the GVV scope. This will not be entirely possible but it needs to be clarified as much as possible from the beginning.

5. *Pedagogy:* The focus then needs to switch quickly from any institutional and process preoccupation on the part of the participants (which is a familiar curse of the public sector), into strategic action. However, even at this point, the instructor needs to acknowledge that all of the appeal and accountability avenues that already exist in the public sector suffer from the weaknesses that have been outlined earlier, and still need to be approached with the tried and tested GVV strategies. It is too often the case that a complainant in the public sector is simply pointed in the direction of the most likely formal complaint avenue or institution, with no formal counseling or advice. Worse still they are simply referred to a website containing a code of ethics and a web address to lodge a formal complaint online.

Then the focus can switch to dynamics and action learning. All of the tried and tested GVV modalities are then useful in the public sector setting, it is just that these strategies may also have to be used in approaching the appeal/complaint bodies themselves, as well as the alleged perpetrators of the offending behavior.

Action learning is best, and case studies are invaluable. Many existing GVV cases are useful even though they relate to the private sector. Here a problem arises in that there are very few existing written GVV cases that occur in a public sector situation. The UQBS project hopes to contribute more but a concerted effort worldwide by academics and practitioners in public administration would be extremely helpful.

The Academic Setting

For educators in an academic setting, the use of GVV in curriculum design and delivery faces the now familiar challenge of the globalization of higher education. A university classroom of students studying public sector management will typically include participants from all or most of the six continents. They come from developed, developing, and emerging economies, encompassing the full range of the political spectrum including democracies, autocracies, totalitarian regimes, and even dictatorships.

Our experience is that their concern about corruption in their home countries increases every year, where international norms are not always recognized especially regarding individual human rights and responsibilities, concepts of rule of law, ethical behavior, and so forth. The separation of powers doctrine is virtually unknown.

Although this may have a marked bearing on the context in which such students receive the messages of a program such as GVV and condition their responsiveness to its basic precepts, educators have to make a fundamental choice to pursue the pure GVV strategy and agenda, endeavoring to see whether there is some way it can be applied in these other cultural settings. For this reason, a number of new GVV cases specifically targeting responses to pervasive corruption in different cultural and business environments have been added to the curriculum over the past year.

It is also the case that many postgraduate students have not had actual work experience in the public sector and so their reaction and impulses will be at the hypothetical level. This is of course a familiar aspect of all tertiary education and should not be an impediment. But it does mean that GVV cases that are written for public sector courses need to have as real a feel about them as possible. Academics in the discipline of public administration/public sector management are already very familiar with this challenge because there are relatively few real-life written case studies available pertaining to public sector experience. Further, GVV public sector cases would also help to rectify this situation and be welcomed by the whole discipline.

The Benefits of Using GVV in the Public Sector

Clearly, providing public servants with the means to identify and analyze the ways in which they can voice and implement their values in the face of countervailing pressure is an important contribution of GVV. By introducing GVV into the public sector management curriculum UQBS helps students and practitioners identify some of the common reasons and rationalizations that can prevent us from acting on our values and discuss ways of overcoming them. The use of real-world examples helps to raise the profile of value-centered conflicts in the day-to-day activities of public servants. This facilitates learning to consider what is at stake for all parties in high-pressure situations and developing a powerful and persuasive response to the rationalizations against speaking up. The incorporation of GVV into the curriculum helps prepare students intending a public sector career to learn to resolve ethical dilemmas and value conflicts in a work setting. The international student cohort at UQBS from governments in developing nations learn that they are not alone in the potential dilemmas they may face when dealing with corruption and they are encouraged, through practice that empowers their capacity to do what they believe is right. Our ambition is to contribute to building public sector cultures, policies, and processes that enable individuals to voice their values.

CHAPTER 7

Developing Negotiation Skills Through the Giving Voice to Values Scripting Approach

Melissa Manwaring

Abstract

The Giving Voice to Values curriculum offers an experiential scripting exercise that is particularly well suited to negotiation courses. The author adapted this exercise for use with a case study on the multiparty negotiations that led to the decision to launch the *Challenger* space shuttle in January 1986. By mapping the relevant stakeholders, articulating what is at stake for each, planning an influence strategy, identifying an initial counterpart, scripting an opening/response/counterresponse, and performing the script, students practice discrete negotiation skills that otherwise may get less attention than they deserve: namely, initiation of a negotiation, development of a coalition-building strategy, and implementing the opening tactic, and influence and persuasion techniques. The exercise also provides a practical, concrete complement to units on ethical dilemmas and ethical decision making. While it has some limitations, the GVV curriculum is likely to align well with most negotiation courses and offers opportunities to fill both substantive and pedagogical gaps.

Keywords

negotiation, scripting, opening, influence, 3-D negotiation, three-dimensional negotiation.

Author Biography

Melissa Manwaring is a faculty member in the Management division at Babson College, where she teaches negotiation at the graduate and undergraduate levels. She also serves as Babson's college-wide director of Institutional Assessment and the education editor for *Negotiation Journal*. A former practicing attorney, trained mediator, and cofounder of the pedagogy initiative at Harvard's Program on Negotiation, she has taught negotiation to thousands of students and clients around the world. Melissa holds a J.D. from Harvard Law School and an M.Ed. from the Harvard Graduate School of Education.

Introduction

Negotiation is a notoriously complex field of study. Negotiation courses and programs have burgeoned over the past several decades;[1] publications and conferences on negotiation education have proliferated;[2] yet negotiation remains challenging to teach and learn.[3] As a field, negotiation is highly interdisciplinary,[4] replete with "wicked problems" and myriad ethical and strategic dilemmas for which there are few right answers.[5] Cultivating negotiation proficiency potentially requires theoretical understanding, behavioral skill development, and the critical examination (and possibly adjustment) of assumptions, mindsets, and habits developed over a lifetime. Successful learning can be difficult to define and even more difficult to measure, particularly over the long term.[6]

Given this complexity, no single teaching approach is sufficient for helping students develop the multifaceted set of capacities required of a skilled negotiator.[7] Accordingly, many negotiation teachers use a range of pedagogical approaches, such as didactic (lectures, presentations, readings), experiential (role simulations, adventure learning), observational (demonstrations, skits, videos), analytical (case studies, hypotheticals), and reflective (debriefing discussions, journals, self- and peer-assessments).[8] Yet, gaps in student learning no doubt remain.

The *Giving Voice to Values* (GVV) curriculum may be helpful in filling some of those gaps. With its focus on what to do after a values-based decision has been made, it is a natural complement to an ethical decision-making unit or course. Less obviously, though, GVV pedagogy can help develop general negotiation skills that apply beyond the context of ethical dilemmas and values-based decisions.

I have adapted the general approach in GVV "Scripts and Skills" module for use in my MBA negotiation course, and discuss below the GVV-based exercise I developed, my pedagogical purposes in doing so, the perceived benefits of this approach, possible limitations of the approach, and additional ways in which negotiation teachers might consider drawing on the GVV curriculum.

Adapting the GVV "Scripts and Skills" Module: Negotiating the *Challenger* Launch

When I initially learned about the GVV curriculum several years ago, I was both intrigued and intimidated. I noticed numerous connections between GVV and negotiation theory and practice, and was interested in using the curriculum. At the same time, I couldn't imagine how to incorporate any additional content into a very full negotiation course, and I was reluctant to cut anything. After consulting with GVV author Dr. Mary Gentile, however, I learned that GVV was intended to be flexible: I could adopt as much or as little as I liked, and *adapt* as needed.

I eventually incorporated a variation of the GVV "Scripts and Skills" module into an existing unit on multiparty negotiation. Rather than dropping anything in order to add GVV, I simply redesigned the unit to integrate elements of GVV content and pedagogy. As part of this unit, prior to my using GVV, students would watch and discuss a video dramatization[9] of the January 27, 1986, negotiation among 32 NASA and Morton Thiokol[10] representatives that resulted in the decision to launch the space shuttle *Challenger* the following morning. As is now well known, *Challenger* exploded shortly after launch due to the failure of the shuttle's O-rings to seal properly in the unusually cold weather. In retrospect, the disaster appears to have been avoidable: Several Morton Thiokol engineers had been concerned about the O-ring safety for some time, and feared that the cold weather would prove problematic, but were unsuccessful in persuading others at Thiokol and NASA to delay the launch. After viewing the launch negotiation video, students would discuss (from a negotiation perspective) what led to the decision to launch and what, if anything, the concerned engineers might have done differently to lead to a different outcome.

My original purposes for this discussion were to develop students' capacities to (a) recognize common multiparty negotiation dynamics and forms of influence in a complex real-life context and (b) develop negotiation strategies from a "3-D" perspective, taking into account behind-the-scenes "setup" moves and deal design considerations as well as the formal communication at the table.[11] While ethical issues sometimes arose during the discussion, ethics and values were not the explicit focus. Nevertheless, I found the *Challenger* case study to be particularly well suited to the GVV approach, because there's no ambiguity over what the right decision was regarding the launch: With the benefit of hindsight, it's clear that the launch on January 28, 1986 was a bad decision. Moreover, at least some stakeholders (Morton Thiokol engineers in particular) were convinced in advance that it would be dangerous to launch that morning due to the unusually cold temperatures. With this set of facts, the exercise is not to determine whether launching was a good or a bad decision, but rather to determine whether and how the concerned engineers might have better "voiced their values" and persuaded other stakeholders to postpone the launch.

I revised this unit by replacing the group discussion with a version of GVV's "Scripts and Skills" module. This module includes several components; I focused on the following two:

- The *Reasons and Rationalizations* exercise in which students identify, script, and articulate (a) the main arguments (i.e., reasons and rationalizations) they need to address in a values-based conflict, (b) what is at stake for the key parties, (c) what levers of influence they might use with those with whom they disagree, (d) their most powerful and persuasive response to the reasons and rationalizations used by those with whom they disagree, and (e) to whom, when, and in what context they should make that response.
- *Guidelines for Peer Coaching* on student scripts developed in the *Reasons and Rationalizations* exercise.

My revised teaching plan for the *Challenger* case study was as follows:

- (Before class) Students are assigned prereadings on influence strategies and "3-D" negotiation.[12] Earlier in the course, students had studied psychological biases in negotiation;[13] they were asked to draw on this background as well.
- (5–10 min) I present a summary of the factual background leading up to the launch negotiations, including the nature of the space shuttle program, the contractual relationship between NASA and Morton Thiokol, Thiokol's modular design of the solid rocket boosters including the O-rings, the history of concerns about O-ring safety, key stakeholders at NASA and Morton Thiokol, the well-publicized "Teacher in Space" program leading to the selection of schoolteacher Christa McAuliffe to join six other astronauts on *Challenger*, the multiple launch delays, and the extremely low predicted temperatures for the revised launch date of January 29, 1986, which led to the 32-person telephone conference among NASA and Thiokol stakeholders in Florida, Texas, and Utah on the evening of January 28. This summary sets the context for the subsequent video.
- (20 min) I show the prelaunch negotiation scenes from the *Challenger* film.[14] The scenes recreate in detail the January 27, 1986, telephone conference among the NASA and Morton Thiokol representatives, instigated at the request of Thiokol engineer Roger Boisjoly. None of the NASA representatives is in the same physical location as the Morton Thiokol representatives, so face-to-face communication occurs only within each organization. Two of the Morton Thiokol engineers (Roger Boisjoly and Arnie Thompson) express concerns about the predicted cold temperatures and recommend delaying the launch. When NASA shuttle program managers Larry Malloy and Stan Reinartz ask for data or reasoning backing up this recommendation, the engineers are unable to persuasively make their case. Data from prior launches are being faxed to NASA during the conference, but appear to be nearly

illegible and not presented in such a way as to illustrate the engineers' concerns. Roger Boisjoly makes the vague and somewhat cryptic statement that it would be "away from goodness" to launch in below-freezing temperatures. George Hardy, NASA's Deputy Director of Science and Engineering, asks whether Morton Thiokol has anything else to transmit. When there is no response, Hardy says that he is "appalled" that Morton Thiokol would at this point in the launch process recommend against a launch, but says that he will not overrule Thiokol's recommendation. Joe Kilminster, Thiokol's vice-president of booster programs, requests a brief caucus offline. During this caucus, Thiokol's senior vice-president Jerry Mason comments that, "We have a management decision as much as an engineering decision" and that "It makes an impression on me when George Hardy says he is appalled at something we recommend." Engineers Boisjoy and Thompson protest briefly that the data suggest it would be unsafe to launch, but they are largely ignored. Mason then tells Bob Lund, Thiokol's vice-president of engineering, to "take off your engineering hat and put on your management hat." Shortly thereafter, the teleconference with NASA resumes and Kilminster informs NASA that Thiokol now recommends proceeding with the launch. George Hardy asks whether anyone has a different opinion. No one says anything. The decision has been made.

- (10–15 min) Students engage in a scripting exercise, based directly on the *Reasons and Rationalizations* exercise. Students form pairs and are given the following instructions:

Imagine you are in the shoes of Morton Thiokol engineer Roger Boisjoly (an engineer with expertise in booster seal joints and the instigator of the prelaunch teleconference). It is two days before the launch. You realize that launch temperatures are forecast to be far below normal. Though you realize the data are inconclusive, you're gravely concerned about the efficacy of the O-rings at low temperatures. You believe the launch should be postponed if temperatures are in fact as low as predicted. Put aside any additional research, tests, and so forth that an engineer might be able to do, and focus on what you could do in terms of negotiation. With your partner, decide:

- *Who are the relevant stakeholders here? What is at stake for each of these parties, including yourself (as Roger Boisjoly)?*

- *Assuming your goal is to postpone the launch until temperatures are warmer, whom would you approach first, and why? Another engineer at Thiokol? Someone higher up within Thiokol management? Someone at NASA? An entire group of stakeholders? Take into account influence strategies as well as 3-D negotiation considerations: What would be the most effective sequence for approaching the other decision makers?*

- *After identifying whom you would approach, imagine you are able to obtain a face-to-face or telephone conversation with that person or persons. Script your opening statement, and think about what else you may want to tell or show them (data, diagrams, and so forth). This should not be just an opening gambit or a self-righteous speech; think strategically about how best to influence the person(s) with whom you're speaking.*

- *Now, imagine the most powerful objections, criticisms, or concerns you might hear in response. What reasons or rationalizations might you hear in favor of proceeding with the launch? Script that out—as powerfully as possible.*

- *Now, script your best response to these objections.*

- (15–20 min) I then select a few pairs to voice their scripts (openings, responses, counterresponses) in front of the class and invite peer feedback: What seems effective, and why? What's less effective, and why? Is there any way to increase the likelihood of influence, whether in the choice of counterpart(s), in the opening, in the counter response, or elsewhere? What do the scripts suggest about the negotiator's assumptions and strategy? (This portion of the exercise is adapted from the *Guidelines for Peer Coaching*).

Each element of this exercise tends to yield rich analysis and reflection. In response to the first question about relevant stakeholders, students generally start by identifying the direct parties to the teleconference (the Morton Thiokol and NASA representatives) and then quickly identify additional parties with much at stake—most notably, the astronauts and their families, and also others such as the Kennedy Space Center (the shuttle launch site), the press and the numerous schoolchildren and teachers around the country who would be watching the shuttle launch live because of the publicity from the Teacher in Space Project. This tends to lead to a broad analysis of what is at stake for these various parties: jobs and careers, money and other tangible resources, personal and organizational reputation, personal and organizational relationships, and—with regard to the astronauts—life or death. Students move beyond their default focus on the parties at the table and their stated concerns to assess the impact of the negotiation on stakeholders *not* at the table, and develop a fuller reckoning of what is truly at stake.

The process of identifying with whom to speak first also fills a gap in typical negotiation courses, which tend to rely heavily on role simulations. In most role simulations, students are simply assigned a role and counterpart(s). In the GVV-based exercise, students have the opportunity to select and sequence their negotiation counterparts—a critical aspect of the away-from-the-table "setup" dimension of negotiation.[15] In identifying whom to approach first, most students have chosen someone within Morton Thiokol—usually either a fellow engineer, on the theory that such a colleague will be easiest to persuade, or someone in the upper management (e.g., Joe Kilminster, Thiokol's vice-president for space booster programs), on the theory that someone higher in the organizational hierarchy will be better able to influence the NASA decision makers. Occasionally, students have chosen to reach out directly to someone at NASA; once, a pair said that they would start by contacting one of the astronauts. The students' choice of who to target first and why can trigger a discussion of coalition building and sequencing strategies: For instance, are they attempting to exploit the patterns of deference by targeting someone who's likely to be able to persuade another key player? Are they sequencing to shape outcome expectations? What are the benefits and limitations of starting the influence campaign with one particular counterpart versus another?

Scripting an opening—response—counter-response allows students to apply their understanding of influence strategies and to engage in perspective taking as they consider what their counterpart's objections might be and how best to address them. In developing their openings, students have leveraged common biases such as loss aversion (highlighting the potential losses—of life, assets, reputation, confidence, and so forth—of an unsuccessful launch) or vividness (describing in vivid detail the possibility of the shuttle exploding on live television with thousands of schoolchildren watching). They have also tried influence techniques such as reframing (pointing out that while the data from prior launches do not prove that launching at the predicted temperatures would be *unsafe*, the standard should be whether the data prove that launching would be *safe*) or the "foot in the door technique" (making a seemingly minor or moderate request such as asking the counterpart to review prior launch data; then building on that commitment with more significant requests such as revising the launch commit criteria).[16]

It's not clear, of course, whether any of the scripts students generate would have changed the outcome, but they might have. At least two Morton Thiokol engineers were convinced that launching the shuttle in such cold weather was the wrong decision, but they were unable to convince others in their own company or at NASA. This exercise allows students to plan both a coalition-building strategy in the "setup" dimension of negotiation and an influence strategy in the interpersonal "table tactics" dimension.[17]

Potential Benefits of the Adapted "Scripts and Skills" Exercise

The potential benefits of incorporating this adapted "Scripts and Skills" exercise into a negotiation course are as follows:

Opportunity to practice initiating a negotiation
The exercise allows students to practice a skill that may be underaddressed in many negotiation courses: Creating and implementing a negotiation opportunity. Negotiations vary greatly in how "standard" or expected they might be. Some types of negotiation are scheduled well in advance, such as a labor–management contract negotiation or a meeting to discuss

settlement of a legal dispute, giving all parties ample notice and time to prepare. Other types of negotiations, such as those regarding a job offer or a car purchase, may be unscheduled, but tend to have typical patterns of interaction on which parties might base their strategies and expectations. In still other situations, a negotiation may arise unexpectedly: A colleague might walk into our office with news about a dramatic change in resources for a joint project, for instance, and we must respond "on the fly" (or walk away or postpone). All of these scenarios offer different challenges regarding preparation and improvisation. One challenge that may not be addressed as frequently, though, is how to initiate a negotiation where none is scheduled or expected.[18] In the "Scripts and Skills" exercise, students practice initiating a negotiation in a situation where negotiation may be unexpected or unprecedented, and where there may be no established patterns of interaction.

Opportunity to practice developing a coalition-sequencing strategy and implementing opening tactics
As a related but a separate benefit, students have the opportunity to practice integrating away-from-the-table strategy with direct, at-the-table interpersonal tactics.[19] Within the space of a relatively brief exercise, students identify a big-picture strategy (What am I trying to accomplish? How will I get there?) and then develop a concrete opening move to implement that strategy. With regard to strategy, this exercise removes some of the artificial borders typical of role simulations: Students are not assigned a particular counterpart or given a specific negotiation environment ("Prepare for your meeting in ___'s office"); rather, as in many real-life situations, they must select their counterpart(s) and create their own negotiation environment. In this sense, the exercise offers situated learning through authentic activity.[20]

Because of their interactive nature, negotiations cannot of course be completely scripted, but particular critical moments can be—at least partially. Negotiators might legitimately script and practice their opening, for instance, as well as their response to a particular question or tactic. Rehearsing and revising openings in response to feedback can be helpful in developing negotiation "micro-skills."[21]

Opportunity to practice influence skills

The exercise also offers an opportunity for students to practice true influence strategies—another skill that may be underaddressed in typical negotiation courses.[22] The goal in this exercise is to figure out how best to influence a set of stakeholders to support a particular decision—which calls for a somewhat different set of negotiation skills than those required to complete a business transaction, settle a legal dispute, or solve a logistical problem. Students go beyond analyzing which influence strategies might have worked ("He should have leveraged loss aversion by highlighting the potential losses" or "They could have capitalized on the vividness bias by describing the risks in detail or creating more compelling visual aids") to actually practicing their influence strategies and receiving feedback.

Opportunity to develop practical skills relating to ethics and values

Ethics and values-based issues are often taught in theoretical terms in the negotiation context—if they are formally taught at all. Various readings offer frameworks for classifying and deciding ethical dilemmas; case studies and hypotheticals offer opportunities for abstract analysis.[23] This approach focuses on skill building: developing a concrete toolkit for *acting* on a values-based decision once it's made, and navigating nonnegotiable values—likely a gap in many negotiation courses.[24]

Observational learning opportunity

Students may benefit not only from creating and performing their scripts, but also from observing those of others. Certainly, the scripted performances provide concrete data on which the class can base its analysis and evaluation. Beyond the data, there may be some learning benefit from observing *skilled* performances (see Nadler et al., 2003). The instructor should try to ensure that at least some of the performed scripts are skillful models, whether through judicious pair selection or through coaching and revision of the scripts.

Potential Limitations of the Exercise

One limitation of the adapted *Scripts and Skills* exercise—though entirely intentional—is that it does not help students decide what is "right" or "fair" or "ethical." The focus is not on the values-based decision; it's on how to take action after such a decision has been made. Many readings, frameworks, exercises, and other materials are available to help students recognize, analyze, and make decisions regarding ethical dilemmas.[25] This particular exercise (and the GVV curriculum generally) is a complement to standard ethics teaching, not a comprehensive replacement (see Gonzalez-Padron et al., 2012).

Another less obvious but possibly more insidious limitation is that students might overextend the assumptions and techniques of the exercise, thus becoming more positional in situations that do not warrant such an approach. Much negotiation theory highlights the limiting nature of entrenched positions, and much prescriptive advice encourages parties to detach from their positions, shift away from assumptions that they are "right," and cultivate an open mindset toward other perspective and other possible negotiated outcomes.[26] The *Scripts and Skills* exercise—and the GVV curriculum generally—starts from the premise that there is no ambiguity about what's "right": That decision has been made, and the challenge is to influence others to support the right decision. While the premise that "I know what's right here" may be appropriate in certain situations, from the *Challenger* launch decision to the numerous scenarios and case studies described in the GVV curriculum, in many other situations this premise is flawed—and potentially a crippling obstacle to understanding and value creation. Given the various biases and heuristics (overconfidence, egocentrism, confirmation, reactive devaluation, and so forth) that tend to encourage entrenched positions regarding what's right, instructors should be careful to contextualize the influence approach in this exercise: it's applicable only *after* a careful analysis of what's "right" in a given situation—if, indeed, the question is even relevant.

Other Possible Applications of GVV to a Negotiation Course

The exercise discussed here is only one example of how a portion of the GVV curriculum might be adapted and incorporated into a negotiation course. With its focus on what to do *after* an ethical decision, GVV is a natural complement to units on ethical dilemmas and ethical decision making. Negotiation is rife with ethical dilemmas, from substantive

(What is a fair outcome?) to procedural (What should I disclose or conceal?) to conflicts of interest (What if my interests are not aligned with my client's or employer's?).[27] Depending on the context (e.g., business school, law school, an international relations program, an executive education workshop), students may explore various ethical rules, frameworks, or guidelines to help them make decisions regarding dilemmas. The "Scripts and Skills" approach to voicing and acting on those decisions provides a bridge between theory and implementation.

Moreover, the "Scripts and Skills" approach might be used in connection with many other negotiation case studies, role simulations, or videos that offer a decision point with an opportunity to speak up with the goal of *persuasion* or *influence*. The GVV curriculum itself includes dozens of cases set in business, academic, intraorganizational, and community contexts, virtually all of which connect in some way to negotiation. But instructors are not limited to the GVV cases. The value of the GVV curriculum to negotiation instructors is not only in the substantive content it offers, but also in the pedagogy. Students do not simply engage in a theoretical discussion about what they would do in a given situation; they create a specific action plan and practice the opening stage of implementing it, with peer and/or instructor feedback. This sort of situated, experiential learning is consistent with the pedagogical approach in many negotiation courses, and may help fill gaps in the development of initiation, sequencing, and influence skills.

CHAPTER 8

The Ethics of Voicing One's Values

Leigh Hafrey

Abstract

"The Ethics of Voicing One's Values" identifies the ethical drivers for the series *Giving Voice to Values* (GVV) itself. I draw first on my experience using GVV in the first-year MBA orientation at the MIT Sloan School of Management, where students discover the importance of a story in management and ethical decision making through "A Tale of Two Stories." I then turn to my experience applying GVV with the MIT Sloan partner programs in China, where it became apparent that the term "values" requires definition and translation, not just abroad, but at home as well. I conclude by suggesting that the characteristics of "good stories"—character, plot, style, reflection—enable the successful application of the lessons of GVV.

Keywords

conversation, character, communication values, Confucianism, cross-cultural norms, ethics, fiction, film, liberal arts, narrative, plot, reflection, story, storytelling, style, translation, values.

Author Biography

Leigh Hafrey since 1995, Hafrey has served as senior lecturer in the Behavioral and Policy Sciences at MIT Sloan School of Management, teaching communication, ethics, and leadership in the MBA and other graduate programs; since 2012, he also coordinates and teaches the 2-year leadership curriculum for the MIT Leaders for Global Operations, an Engineering/ MBA dual-degree program. Hafrey is senior moderator for the Aspen Institute, where he leads seminars for programs in the United States and abroad. A former staff editor at *The New York Times Book Review*, Hafrey has published translations from French and German and reporting, essays, reviews, and interviews in *The New York Times* and other periodicals. His book on how people use story to articulate ethical norms, *The Story of Success: Five Steps to Mastering Ethics in Business*, appeared in 2005.

Introduction: Giving Voice to Values and Ethics Instruction

I adopted Mary Gentile's Giving Voice to Values (GVV) in the classroom for the same reason that many others have: I needed something that would allow both me and my students in various graduate business programs to ground the metaphysics of our ethical debates in action. I had taught communication, ethics, corporate social responsibility, and a rudimentary version of what we now call sustainability for close to 20 years. Mary and I had become acquainted in the late 1980s at Harvard Business School (HBS). We shared a scholarly humanities background, training that I had never anticipated applying in the service of better corporate performance. Two decades later, the liberal—and even the literary—arts have taken a lead position in forging the link between business practice and the larger social good.

At HBS, Mary and I led sections of the child psychiatrist and Harvard professor Robert Coles' popular course "The Business World: Moral and Social Inquiry Through Fiction." Bob's approach—applying stories to the question of ethics in business—felt like a positive step away from one predicated on comparing and contrasting "deontology" and "consequentialism": We talked about real people in real situations (or at least, fictionally real people in fictionally plausible situations), taking steps to alter their often dire circumstances. Beyond Aristotle's unities of action, place, and time, good stories helped individuals and their organizations identify perennial challenges to our sense of right and wrong, however new the economic circumstances under which we met them. For Coles, such works as Arthur Miller's *Death of a Salesman* or William Carlos Williams' novel *White Mule* made the connection to our MBAs' concerns; I expanded those choices into the realm of modern film and more foreign fiction.

Little did I know then that other, even more concrete possibilities for ethics instruction lay ahead, thanks to Mary's persistence in addressing how people can use a story to make the right choice, rather than merely recognize the complexity of doing so. In the following pages, I will draw first on my experience with GVV at the MIT Sloan School of Management, where I have taught since 1995, to identify the intersection of narrative and ethics in GVV. During a recent Academy of Management session on the series, Mark Edwards, a lecturer in Management and Organizations at the University of Western Australia, commented: "GVV is about conversations. This is the heart of GVV—developing and practicing conversations." He might have added that every conversation is driven by the fundamental human instinct to tell stories. In conversation, we test for the narrative that will allow us to connect, and then join, with other people in building the norms by which we live.

At the same time, the give-and-take of conversation makes us take seriously the inevitable otherness of our audience(s), and so attend to new possibilities, even as we confirm our chosen response. After exploring briefly the narrative core of GVV, I will describe my use of the series in graduate business programs at several Asian schools, to illustrate the necessity—even at home—of naming or locating the values that we believe should drive our behavior, in order then consciously to dis- or relocate them. The conversation about "the right thing to do" too often runs aground on assumptions about what we believe, in the absence of a recognition that we routinely translate our notions of right and wrong for others, even those who speak our mother tongue. The "good stories" that keep us honest do so by offering answers, yet simultaneously suggesting other possibilities: We make our rigorously "right" decisions in the face of an uncertainty that forces us, as GVV itself requires, into a permanently vigilant, ethically exploratory stance. Thus are narrative and ethics joined.

Teaching GVV at MIT Sloan: From Threat to Inspiration—The Story Factor

In the wake of the scandals at Enron, WorldCom, Global Crossing, and other companies at the beginning of the century, MIT Sloan's ethics programming became a central feature of our orientation week, the mandatory 4-day introduction to the School and its offerings for the entering class of MBA's. Between 2003 and 2008, that programming evolved significantly. On the down side, we needed to account for the bursting of the dot-com bubble, various high-profile corporate failures, and then the subprime mortgage debacle, the consequences of which we still face today. More positively, our efforts had to match a rising interest in standards among the last Gen X and leading-edge Millennials, the then 20-somethings who were bringing high expectations and, often, high ideals to the business workplace. While Boomer employers, having once distrusted everyone over 30, might now bemoan the work ethic of anyone under that age (more often than not, their own offspring), the demand for conversation about ethics, corporate social responsibility, and sustainability appeared to be rising.

Early in this evolution, we used fairly traditional materials at MIT Sloan: the HBS best-selling case/article by Bowen McCoy, "The Parable of the Sadhu"; a long and prescient chapter by Richard Locke, faculty at MIT Sloan and in MIT's political science department, "Nike: Globalization and the Evolution of Corporate Citizenship"; the UN Global Compact; the Instituto de Empresa's "Proposed Hippocratic Oath for Business," and ethics vignettes and caselets written by students, based on their own experience. Student evaluations of the material registered an appreciation of its relevance, but skepticism about its utility, given—as so many respondents said—that compliance with any set of ethical standards would be voluntary.

In order to put teeth into our principles, I steered us toward what I now think of as an "enforcer" mentality. Our primary instructor in business law taught several sessions synchronized to the ethics discussions, and we linked both to sessions on professional standards: How we expected our students to behave at Sloan, in and out of the classroom. After a year or two, it became clear that tying social justice to eating in class did a disservice to both engagements, and so we began thinking about how to manage a turn from enforcement to inspiration. Sloan's Career Development Office had articulated an approach to career planning that focused on students telling their "story," and the requisite Orientation session on the case method sounded the same note. When I serendipitously discovered GVV's "A Tale of Two Stories," we had a full-day sequence built around the role that story plays in our business and personal lives, and within those stories, the values that drive us, our organizations, and our culture.

Did we revolutionize ethics instruction at Sloan? Given that various faculty had used story to address values in and out of the workplace well before I arrived in the mid-1990s, probably not. We did now have a coherent conceptual framework, though, one that in the next year or two allowed us to reach back to Day 1 of Orientation, where we focused on the School's mission to "develop principled, innovative leaders," mediated by the Sloan faculty's Four Capabilities Leadership Model. We also reached forward to our keynote speaker on Day 4, the protagonist from the case we had done mid-week, who now joined us to tell his or her "story." It wasn't essential that the MBA's see the wiring to this machine but that they feel they had access to a consistent set of messages about how to focus and act on values.

In 2010, we expanded both our ethics programming and our use of GVV, launching a mandatory four-session module titled "Ethics, Values, and Voice." "EVV" included a case on sustainability and a panel on ethics in finance, and it built on our use in Orientation of "A Tale of Two Stories," asking students to choose one of the stories they told in their teams then, and develop it into a skit. In line with the series' emphasis on "scripting" the language and action necessary to speak up for one's values, the associated attention to recognizing and resisting dissuasive counterarguments—"reasons and rationalizations"—and the importance of peer coaching, we took the story principle a step further, building out the narrative component to ethical action and adding a performance element; we now had drama (not always seen as a plus in business settings!), together with the hands-on practicality that distinguishes GVV and links to Sloan's emphasis on skills and action learning. Student response to the scripting exercise was very positive, and led us to continue it.

Teaching GVV in Asia: Finding a Voice

I first went to China in 2001, under the auspices of the MIT-China Management Education Project. The program began in 1996, with an agreement between MIT and Tsinghua University in Beijing and Fudan University in Shanghai; in 1999, the program expanded to include Lingnan (University) College at Zhongshan University, in Guangzhou.

At Tsinghua, Fudan, and Zhongshan Universities, the schools established English-language International MBA programs, designed to help build a cadre of young business people who understood global business practices. At Sloan, we worked with visiting faculty from the schools, helping them to do the research and design the curricula they needed to meet program goals; we also sent Sloan faculty, and then student teams, to visit our Chinese counterparts.

On my first visit to China, I brought an internationalist curriculum in business ethics and leadership, including materials from America, Ireland, Japan, and Germany. That range had worked at HBS and MIT Sloan, where the students came from all over the globe; in the classroom, someone always had local knowledge of the world of the story, no matter how geographically remote. The variety enabled the class to proceed to a comparison of local standards and arguably cross-cultural norms, grounding the familiar debate about ethics as "situational" or "absolute" not in abstraction, but the realities of cultural difference and professional alignment.

My Chinese students both needed and wanted something else, though. They wanted to learn the norms that govern American business, and jettison their "Chinese values." They were enormously enthusiastic, and cordial, and outspoken about their need to learn the ways of the West in order to enter the global marketplace. In their late 20s, and enrolled in both full-time and part-time programs, they showed the fire and can-do attitude I knew from their American peers; as we chatted in the class and on the tours of local sites that they hosted for me, though, they made it clear that they felt a parochialism requiring radical solutions.

In response to their vehement purpose, I jettisoned the multicultural agenda I had originally carried, and simply asked: "What *are* Chinese values?" The answer came back, equally simple: "We are a Confucian society." No one suggested that the People's Republic of China was a Communist society; no one initially mentioned the Cultural Revolution, which had targeted so much of traditional Chinese society, destroying many physical testimonials to those traditions. We talked a fair amount about the weight of the West on China over the preceding century and a half, about China's "submissiveness," and the West's "missionary impulse," but that juxtaposition didn't seem to mitigate the students' desire to buy into the ideology of the capitalist marketplace.

I have written elsewhere about my early attempts to determine the place and significance of Confucian values in 21st-century China.[1] For several years, I taught Confucius there, initially pairing *The Analects* with Aristotle's *Politics* to show points of convergence and divergence East and West. What matters here is that, when I finally brought "A Tale of Two Stories" to China, my Chinese IMBA's made it clear that we needed to have a conversation about values, *to name them* before we started talking about how we stood up for them.

By then, a number of factors had changed the tenor of our discussions. The partner IMBA programs had become modestly international in their demographics: A small percentage of the students now came from the United States, Latin America, or Europe, and a significant number from South Korea. Perhaps because of this influx, the Chinese students had turned somewhat laconic in class, even as China's admission to the World Trade Organization and its successful bid for the 2008 Olympics increased national pride and self-confidence, generating what one of my American colleagues referred to as "the new muscular nationalism."

Now, when I asked the lead question in a session built around GVV's "A Tale of Two Stories," "What do we mean when we talk about values?" more often than not a Westerner would raise a hand and offer "fairness," or "trust," or "honesty." And then, after a few more such exploratory moves, a Chinese student would propose "humanity," "reciprocity," "filial piety"—the building blocks of the Confucian system. When that happened, and when I pointed out the source of the contribution, the floodgates would open to a dozen related terms, and a sudden ease of self-recognition among the Chinese participants. While they might still dream of a cowboy-capitalist ethos, they appeared to have come to terms with a truth I had tried to impart in previous years: One doesn't simply eradicate values; if the cadres of the Cultural Revolution hadn't succeeded in the endeavor, mild-mannered business faculty would hardly do better.

In the end, that comfort, more than anything else, has led me to ask the same question with my Sloan and other audiences, with or without a GVV text before us. Ethics instructors will likely recognize my experience of working with people who declare that they know their values, but are hard put to label them when pressed to do so. This doesn't reveal an absence of values, I think, but rather, a reluctance to express them in a context where competing values might come into play, or where a pragmatic focus on getting things done—a very business mindset—seems to proscribe conversation with metaphysical or (in something of a conceptual contradiction) emotional overtones. Perhaps the confusion or reticence also stems from a classificatory challenge: For example, is "democracy" a value, or a mechanism for fulfilling a set of values? For my Chinese students, is "humanity" a value, or a relic of a system that no longer obtains in a world where the market apparently sets the norm, *is* the norm?

In both cases, voicing the values at stake is a first and necessary step toward appreciating the possibility of difference and disagreement, and with it the push toward consensus that must underlie any code of ethics. This translation effort seems fundamental, not just to the conversation about ethics, but to speaking up for our values, as GVV asks us to do. We do not act in a void, and while the reality of community and conformity can bring with it the "reasons and rationalizations" we need to decipher and resist, when we sketch cultural and psychological circumstances we can sometimes advance, rather than retard, our capacity for doing the right thing. Taken from a 90–120" exercise, that 10 minutes of naming our values has since become standard for me wherever I use "A Tale of Two Stories," because the cosmopolitanism that I perceived and to which I catered in the West only masked a similar disjunction.

Conclusion: GVV Preaches Communication Values

In the GVV note "Ways of Thinking about Our Values in the Workplace," Mary Gentile draws on the late ethicist Rushworth Kidder's writing to offer a common set of values. As the earlier discussion will have indicated, my teaching experience with GVV suggests that another set of values shapes both the project and its yield. These are communication values, which—like democracy or humanity—are intended to mediate "honesty, respect, responsibility, fairness and compassion."[2] At their heart lies narrative, the perennial human impulse to tell a story, build a logical suite of events that allows us to make sense, for us and others, of what we have done, are doing, and still hope to do. To make that narrative possible, we also need—and here my experience in China bears on the GVV enterprise—the vocabulary of values to drive us to the ethical fulfillment that the series promises.

What does it mean to live in a world determined by the narrative impulse? It means sometimes resisting "the facts," the terms on which life seems available to most of us most of the time. Early in Paul Rusesabagina's book, *An Ordinary Man: an Autobiography*, Rusesabagina explains that "words" were both the drivers for the genocide in Rwanda in 1994, and the means by which he rescued 1,268 Tutsi and moderate Hutu refugees in the hotel that he had managed before the violence began.[3] In that sense, of course, the communication values that I invoke here become a double-edged sword: Narrative heightens the effect of our intent, but does not dictate its good or evil quality. For that, we need Kidder's values; we may also need the test of faith; and we certainly need the regulation provided by the notion of "a good story."

GVV puts the components of a good story on the table, asking us to concentrate on our own and others' humanity. Those components include:

1. **Character**: In the cases, and in exercises such as "A Tale of Two Stories," the series acknowledges the complex agendas that individuals may bring to a community, the "reasons and rationalizations" that can thwart our values-driven intentions, as well as the principles that help us persevere.

2. **Plot**: Our aims generate the action, a plot conditioned by events that often escape the individual actor's control, but are susceptible to his or her response. In responding, we hope to control a situation, set and maintain the standard by which we wish to live.

3. **Style**: GVV catalogues the rhetorical devices ("scripts and skills") and organizational language that we use to achieve our storybook ends. The "voice" of GVV reprises Rusesabagina and my Chinese students' need to find and use the right words.

4. **Reflection**: GVV's emphasis on scripts turns storytelling into a reflexive exercise. The salutary value of the scripted story lies in its combination of familiarity and artistic distance, assuming and then reframing our sense of what is right for others and our selves.

When students share their workplace experience in GVV's "A Tale of Two Stories," they and their fellows in the small-group exercise are looking for a voice that not only speaks to values, but also speaks from them. How ethical is a good story? Toward the end of *An Ordinary Man*, Rusesabagina invokes the novelist and lay theologian C.S. Lewis to set the norms for our existence, in defiance of the evil that he witnessed in Rwanda: "No, the true state of human affairs is life as it *ought to be lived*."[4] In and out of the hospitality industry, where Rusesabagina had chosen to make his career, that seems the best possible standard on which to engage with the world.

CHAPTER 9

Voicing Values in Pursuit of a Social Mission

The Role of Giving Voice to Values in Social Entrepreneurship Teaching

Denise Crossan

Abstract

The number of undergraduate and postgraduate courses being taught in the area of nonprofit management and social entrepreneurship has seen unprecedented growth in the past 6 to 7 years.[1] At the same time and as a perceived response to the global economic crisis, commercial business courses have increased their focus in areas such as corporate social responsibility.[2] While the teaching of ethics as a subject in the commercial business curriculum has been commonplace for the past three to four decades, the teaching of ethics as a component of a social entrepreneurship curriculum remains relatively rare. Therefore, this chapter will explore the application of Giving Voice to Values (GVV) pedagogy within a social entrepreneurship curriculum, giving examples of GVV for social entrepreneurship case materials developed for MBA students in a business school.

Keywords

social entrepreneurship, social enterprise, nonprofit, social economy sector, social mission, social entrepreneurship curriculum.

Author Biography

Dr. Denise Crossan was appointed to Trinity College Dublin's School of Business in January 2009 as assistant professor in Social Entrepreneurship; the first post of its kind in Ireland. She acts as TCD Director for the Initiative on Social Entrepreneurship, teaching undergraduate and postgraduate courses and carrying out research in the areas of social enterprise and social entrepreneurship nationally and internationally. Dr. Crossan's in-field experience includes assisting community groups to establish social businesses under the European Union's Special Programme for Peace and Reconciliation in Northern Ireland from 1996 to 2002 and establishing her own consultancy business in 2002 to support social enterprises in Northern Ireland and the Republic of Ireland.

Introduction

The number of undergraduate and postgraduate courses being taught in the area of nonprofit management and social entrepreneurship has seen unprecedented growth for the past 6 to 7 years.[3] This growth in interest has been explained by David Bornstein as simply due to the fact that "more people today have the freedom, time, wealth, exposure, social mobility, and confidence to address social problems in new ways."[4] At the same time, unprecedented attention has been given in recent years to the perceived lack of social responsibility being exercised by corporate business globally, dramatically exposed by the current global recession.[5] As students become increasingly disenfranchised with the perceived irresponsible actions of the commercial business world, it would appear that more seek to learn about business that creates wealth, while at the same time creating positive measurable social impact. As a result, this increased desire to tackle the roots of social and environmental injustice has created a demand for appropriate educational curriculum to support student learning.[6] As the majority of social entrepreneurship courses are taught in business schools, a blurring of the divide between courses related to purely for-profit goals and courses related to nonprofit goals has become increasingly evident.

While the teaching of ethics as a subject in the commercial business curriculum has been commonplace for the past three to four decades, the teaching of ethics as a component of a social entrepreneurship curriculum remains relatively rare. This may be in part due to the newness of teaching social entrepreneurship courses in general (only coming to prominence within the past 10 years or so) and also in part due to the emphasis on using stellar case studies (such as Muhammad Yunus, Grameen Bank) as the main mechanism for teaching. Some authors[7] reflect that the very nature of social entrepreneurship as an activity (in essence, business that seeks to achieve social goals over financial profit) suggests that there may be less of a need to teach ethics as a component of a social entrepreneurship course due to its intentional pursuit of good for society.

However, in recent times, our teaching of social entrepreneurship has evolved from the application of qualitative exemplar cases in the field, to a more management- and complexity-focused analysis of the behavior and performance of social entrepreneurs in practice. Developing social entrepreneurship curriculum now seeks to consider our understanding of the actions required to successfully achieve a social mission and measureable social impact, as well as a more quantitative analysis on the enablers and barriers, including ethical challenges, which affect the journey of the social entrepreneur.

Therefore, the purpose of this chapter is to explore the application of Giving Voice to Values (GVV) pedagogy within a social entrepreneurship curriculum. The chapter will refer directly to the experience of teaching GVV for social entrepreneurship case materials developed for MBA students in a business school.

It is worth reiterating that the field of social entrepreneurship is relatively new and academic courses in social entrepreneurship and research on ethical challenges facing social entrepreneurs is also relatively underdeveloped. Therefore, the beginning sections of the chapter will give a brief definition of social entrepreneurship and an overview of the research that explores the unique nature of ethical challenges faced by social entrepreneurs. Following this, the GVV for social entrepreneurship pedagogy will be examined and discussed.

Defining Social Entrepreneurship

Defining the Concept

Although there is no one singular definition for the term social entrepreneurship, for the most part, commentators agree that social entrepreneurs are individuals who, having identified a social mission as their primary purpose, employ a business model to generate income that supports the achievement of the social mission.[8] Similar to social entrepreneurs, a social enterprise is an enterprise created and managed by a group of people who are working collectively toward the achievement of a common social mission. While both the social entrepreneur and the social enterprise adopt business models and mechanisms to generate income for their respective activities, the surplus income raised by either is typically reinvested in activities and programs to realize the social mission, or reinvested back into the enterprise to ensure its sustainability in the long term.[9] Most importantly, the social mission is the driving force of both the social entrepreneur and the social enterprise, and theoretically, all decisions made with regard to the business are made with a view to moving toward the overall achievement of the social mission.

It is important to note that social entrepreneurs/enterprises represent only one form of a highly diverse range of organization structures that follow the principle of prioritizing their social mission over the maximization of the financial bottom line. Other organizational forms (such as associations, foundations, cooperatives, credit unions, and trusts) often referred to as nonprofit, not for profit, or third sector organizations are typically categorized, along with social entrepreneurs and social enterprises, as contained within the social economy sector.[10] The social economy sector is often described as the sector operating in the space between the public and private sectors.

Increasingly, as the global economy suffers from ongoing recession and governments seek alternative mechanisms for the delivery of public services, the organizations within the social economy, including social entrepreneurs, have become recognized as key agents in the delivery of public sector services internationally.[11] Likewise, with increased competitiveness between the social economy sector and the private sector for lucrative government contracts, increasingly social entrepreneurs and social enterprises are being shaped by an agenda to "professionalize, commercialize or perish."[12]

Origins of the Social Mission: Values and Beliefs

The importance of the social mission to the social entrepreneur and social enterprise cannot be overstated. Indeed, research has shown that the identity of the organization, its ethos, and day-to-day operations are highly determined by the pivotal beliefs, values, and sense of identity of the person or people involved in the creation and ongoing management of the social enterprise.[13] Furthermore, research has shown that employees and volunteers, who chose to engage with a social enterprise, do so after very careful evaluation of the relation between the organization's social mission and their own personal beliefs and values.[14]

Given that the origins of the social mission are intrinsically linked to the personal identity and value systems of the founder, manager, and employees, any conversation around ethical behavior for social entrepreneurs must take into account the genesis and articulation of the values and beliefs of the individuals within the enterprise. As shown later, the voicing of values through the GVV process and the articulation of the social mission are closely linked, and make GVV an excellent mechanism to support students in identifying, honing, and articulating their values and social mission.

Ethical Challenges in Social Entrepreneurship

Just as the spotlight highlighted unethical practice on a grand scale within the commercial business sector in recent years, similarly highly regarded, high-profile nonprofit organizations have been hit hard by unethical practice scandals.[15] In fact, research from the 1990s shows that in a survey carried out among nonprofit chief executives, 80 percent dealt with ethical issues in the workplace on a regular basis.[16]

The reality facing the social entrepreneur and social enterprise is that the dichotomous nature of their enterprise operations (working toward a primary social purpose while at the same time acting as a business) creates a myriad of complex ethical challenges. Research in this area has identified ethical challenges and behaviors that are considered common from a general business context, and has also shown evidence of ethical challenges that are highly context specific to social entrepreneurs and social enterprises.[17] Therefore, in this section, examples of the nature of these ethical challenges, both common and sector specific, will be briefly examined.

Research on the nature of unethical practice in nonprofits has shown that individuals working in social enterprise are just as likely to engage in unethical behavior, and typical examples identified include actions such as:[18]

- mismanagement of enterprise assets for personal gain;
- theft of cash or inventory from the enterprise;
- "kickback schemes" for individuals or associated private organizations; and
- fraudulent statements or falsification of financial and nonfinancial reports.

Indeed, some authors suggest that the very egotistical nature of the entrepreneur (similarly displayed in the social entrepreneur), which allows them to take risks and be extremely persuasive in influencing others, can leave them open to acting unethically in certain circumstances.[19] The unethical behaviors outlined previously are typically driven by the individual with little regard for the long-term consequences on the social enterprise or the community. They represent conscious or subconscious actions of malpractice and are only one layer of the type of the potential ethical challenges facing a social enterprise.

In the field, social entrepreneurs are often depicted as champions of a cause, radical thinkers, challengers of the status quo, and, in some cases, depicted as "rule breakers."[20] In social entrepreneurship, there is a certain amount of acceptance (and applause) of the mindset that if you want to destroy old and inherently unjust systems then you must be bold and push the boundaries of acceptable behavior in order to change the current regime. In doing so, when faced with an ethical dilemma, a social entrepreneur may rationalize his or her actions by applying a differentiation between doing something that is "wrong and is for personal gain," versus doing something "wrong that is for the collective gain of the beneficiaries" of the social mission. It is within this context that the potential for social entrepreneurship sector-specific ethical challenges are most anticipated and where commentators point out that social entrepreneurs might "contradict the known ethical principle that the end cannot, and should not, justify the means."[21]

The following scenarios based on recent research[22] aim to illustrate two examples of sector-specific ethical dilemmas faced by social entrepreneurs:

In the first example, the social entrepreneur, a nonprofits consultant, is asked to carry out a financial evaluation of a community organization that assists individuals with severe disabilities in claiming government living support payments. The social entrepreneur realizes that the applications being made by the organization are exaggerating the client's disabilities in order to secure the highest statutory living support payment amount. The social entrepreneur believes that this exaggeration is wrong, indeed, fraud; however, she also realizes that if she speaks out against the practice, the clients of the organization will ultimately lose out the much needed financial payments in order to keep their living standards above the poverty line. Also, the community organization's good reputation will be ruined. If she doesn't speak out, and later the details of the fraud are uncovered, her own reputation as a nonprofit consultant could be ruined.

In the second example, the social entrepreneur, confronted with a donor funding cash flow crisis, is faced with the decision whether to write salary checks for his employees, with the knowledge that the social enterprise does not have the funds in the bank to cover the checks. In addition, as a board member must also sign the checks, the social entrepreneur not only considers breaking the law, but through withholding the dire financial information, may cause the board member to break the law also. The social entrepreneur knows that this action is wrong; however, he also realizes that many of the employees expecting their salaries are the social beneficiaries of the organization; coming from the target low-income community that the enterprise's social mission aims to ultimately support. Not receiving their salaries could have devastating consequences for the vulnerable employees.

In the first example, the community organization is involved in activities that, although fraudulent, are being done in pursuit of the greater good for their beneficiaries; individuals who would not be able to receive financial assistance without the intervention of the community organization. The social entrepreneur realizes the impact that the withdrawal of financial support would have if she were to not go along with the fraudulent activity. In the second example, the social entrepreneur feels compelled to act unethically in order to ensure the support of his social enterprise's primary beneficiaries, the employees. In both cases, the social entrepreneurs are faced with the ethical challenge that they might frame as "doing bad in order to do good"; a particularly salient challenge for the social entrepreneur and social enterprise.

Ethics, GVV, and the Social Entrepreneurship Curriculum

As stated earlier, majority of social entrepreneurship courses are currently delivered in a business school environment and up until very recently, the curriculum for social entrepreneurship has been highly influenced by an emphasis on the business start-up aspect of social enterprise. Therefore, a curriculum for a social entrepreneurship course might typically contain the following elements:

- historical origins of social entrepreneurship/social enterprise;
- the organizational landscape of the social economy or classification of social enterprises;
- analysis of the difference between a commercial entrepreneur and a social entrepreneur such as characteristics, traits, and environment;
- starting a social enterprise; business and strategic planning;
- review of operational issues such as legal structures, governance, financial management, marketing, human resource management (including managing volunteers), operations management; and
- measurement of impact or the "double bottom line."

Often the primary pedagogy would be qualitative examples of social entrepreneurs in the field through case studies.

More recently, as the subject of social entrepreneurship becomes more informed by qualitative and quantitative research data, curricula for social entrepreneurship courses have begun to reflect a more management-focused approach to understanding the key facets of social entrepreneurship, and so the following topics are being integrated into courses:

- the genesis of the social mission and its importance to the behavior of the social enterprise;
- understanding the decision-making processes of social entrepreneurs reflecting both the social and economic needs of the enterprise; and
- identifying enablers or barriers to social entrepreneurship development in a particular environment.

The conversation around ethics and ethical challenges faced by social entrepreneurs is not currently overtly covered by social entrepreneurship curriculum in general. However, values and beliefs play an important part in the elements of curriculum discussing the identification and creation of a social mission. Likewise, when discussing enablers and barriers to social entrepreneurship development, the area of values, beliefs, and active ethical awareness is also touched upon in a few examples.

As the social entrepreneurship curriculum evolves from simply applying a traditional business curriculum structure to a perceived new genre of business, social entrepreneurship teachers are being challenged to find mechanisms that help students articulate their own personal values and beliefs. This new mechanism would allow students to construct their social mission from the understanding of their values, and then build an appropriate business model that allows the student to enact their social mission first, and then their financial goals as a secondary objective.

This is where the GVV curriculum becomes a vital tool for the social entrepreneurship teacher. The Giving Voice to Values (GVV) curriculum sets the student a series of exercises, questionnaires, cases, and discussion questions based on seven core principles or "Pillars," which work cumulatively to assist students in identifying, articulating, practicing, and voicing their core values and beliefs in times of challenge.[23] These exercises are highly aligned with desired aspects of a social entrepreneurship curriculum. It is possible to apply the GVV curriculum as a framework for the student of social entrepreneurship to explore their own personal values and beliefs, and then translate their findings into a social mission for their enterprise. Therefore, GVV for social entrepreneurship allows students to practice voicing their values/social mission throughout the life of their social entrepreneurial journey, identifying the enablers and barriers to staying true to their social mission and practice their social values voice.

By way of example of how GVV can be applied to a social entrepreneurship course, the remainder of this chapter aims to describe an example of a GVV for social entrepreneurship class delivered to MBA students, where the students were required to consider the ethical challenges facing social entrepreneurs, and to practice how they might respond and voice their values in similar scenarios.

The Classroom Experience: GVV for Social Entrepreneurship

Having been asked to teach a class on social entrepreneurship as part of a 12-week "Business in Society" course for MBA students, it was agreed that the class should cover an introduction to the topic of social entrepreneurship, talk about how social entrepreneurs pursue the social mission over profit, and then focus on the types of challenges (including ethical) they might face in the process. Although not strictly a dedicated program for postgraduate students on either social entrepreneurship or nonprofit management, the MBA students would later in their program take part in a full-service learning-styled course on social entrepreneurship that would require them to work with social entrepreneurs directly in the field. The class discussion on challenges faced by social entrepreneurs would act as a precursor to their fuller service learning course on social entrepreneurship.

As the class was scheduled for only 2 hours and given the objective of preparing students for their in-field experience, it was decided the most appropriate elements of the GVV curriculum would be a GVV-style case discussion plus the exercises, "A Tale of Two Stories: The Power of Choice."[24]

Based on the research on sector-specific ethical challenges faced by social entrepreneurs as discussed previously, case studies were developed that articulated such ethical conflicts.[25] The case used for the MBA class was based on the first scenario described earlier (the consultant was called "Caroline"). The case consisted of a part A and part B, with questions for reflection at the end of each section. In part A, students were presented with the scenario and the core aspects of the ethical challenge faced by the social entrepreneur. In part B, the case discussed the action taken by the social entrepreneur to voice her values.

The subsequent "Tale of Two Stories" exercise is based on the premise that in normal daily interactions within organizations, managers are faced with ethical challenges on a regular basis. This exercise invites students to reflect on the fact that, on some occasions, managers find ways to voice and enact their values, and at other times, they may fail to do so, and one can learn from this reflection to optimize their capacity for the former.

From a delivery perspective, the class consisted of approximately 25 mature MBA students, all of whom had a minimum 5 years of work experience at a senior management level, predominantly within the private sector. The class delivery structure was divided into three stages. In the first stage, students were asked to form small groups of five or six members and to discuss part A of the case study. Then students were asked to reflect on set questions and respond. In the second stage, students were asked to read and consider part B of the case, and then reflect on the case questions and discuss. In the third stage of the class, students were asked to work independently, and to take some time to think about times when in their own work experience they faced an ethical dilemma (based on "A Tale of Two Stories"). Students were then given the option of discussing the ethical challenge they faced openly with the class, and to describe what action they took to overcome the challenge; what motivated them to speak out, or perhaps prevented them from speaking out; what factors enabled or disabled them from speaking out and how satisfied they were with the outcome overall.[26] Students were asked to consider how the experiences reflected on what they believed were their own personal social values.

Having read and discussed part A of the case study in their groups, students were asked to identify what they thought were the core elements of Caroline's ethical dilemma. Each group contributed to the discussion and without much debate was able to agree the following core aspects of the case:

- The activities of the community organization are tantamount to government fraud;
- Caroline knows that the activity of the community organization is wrong;

- However, if she speaks out against the practice:
  - the beneficiaries of the nonprofit organization would suffer in loss of income;
  - the community organization's reputation would be ruined;
  - other funders might withdraw their financial support; and
  - Caroline's reputation as a consultant may also be damaged.

When the students were asked "What should Caroline do?" The class response was split equally, with 50 percent immediately and quite adamantly stating that Caroline should report the fraudulent activity immediate to the government agency. Their rationale for this decision was that Caroline was not responsible to the community organization, or their clients, and as a tax payer, she had a moral obligation to ensure that only those who truly meet the criteria for living support payments should receive them. The other 50 percent of the class was more undecided and hesitant to respond immediately. Slowly they began to provide arguments as to why Caroline should not report the fraud. Their rationalizations for not speaking out ranged from "It's not her problem so she shouldn't get involved," "She only needs to report the good work of the community organization and she could tailor her report to that information only," to "No one should allow people with severe disabilities to suffer because the government doesn't want to give them enough money to live. I am glad the community organization is behaving this way," to finally "Caroline shouldn't sell out her community."

In a true GVV class discussion, the question would not be "What should Caroline do?," but rather "Given that Caroline knows the organization is engaged in fraudulent reporting, how can she enact her values most effectively and responsibly?" This question engages the students in working actively to generate scripts and action plans for acting on their values, rather than rationalizing the failure to do so. Although the approach here was slightly different, the discussion did move to the true GVV question as students came to define Caroline's ethical challenges as the following:

1. How could she voice what she believes is ethically right?
2. How can she ensure her professional reputation remains intact?
3. How can she follow her social mission? and,

4. As a social entrepreneur, how can she ensure that her decision does not impinge negatively on either the community organization or their beneficiaries?

These questions are clearly about finding an action plan for ethical behavior rather than about a purely intellectualized ethical debate, and it is this action-orientation that distinguishes GVV from more traditional ethical pedagogies.

At the end of part A, the students recognize that both Caroline and the manager of the community organization were faced with a sector-specific ethical challenge where their rationalization of the situation might lead them to act in an unethical way in order to pursue some perceived higher good, not for themselves, but for the collective gain of others—the "doing bad to do good" phenomena of the social entrepreneur. At this point, the students were heavily engaged in debate around "doing bad to do good" and offered other examples of where this challenge can arise within social enterprise contexts.

In part B, students were able to read how Caroline decided to voice her values. Students learned that through dialogue with both the government agency and the community organization, Caroline was able to find an agreement on the flawed nature of the application process for receiving government living support payments. Through her intervention, discussion, and recommendation, Caroline was able to negotiate a way forward that would allow the community organization and the government agency to work more collaboratively together in future to collectively meet the needs of the beneficiaries better. Students discussed the actions taken by Caroline and agreed the following important steps in her being able to voice her values, such as:

1. having a strong conscious sense of her own ethical values and beliefs;
2. having a clear social mission, which focused on improving the lives of others;
3. having a good working relationship with both the government agency and the community organization; and
4. having a mechanism, such as her evaluation report, where she could make recommendations for better practice.

In stage 3 of the class, the MBA students, having considered the case study's ethical dilemma from a social entrepreneurship perspective, were asked to then consider their own experiences and identify a time where they may have faced an ethical challenge in a difficult situation. Students were asked to think about the event, to describe the context and potential consequences; what their actions were; what enabled their response or acted as barriers to moving forward; and finally if they were happy with the outcome. Students were asked to work independently and were told that sharing their findings with the class was made optional. Approximately one-third of the class was willing to share their experiences. Students relayed events where they were asked to behave in a manner that they felt was unethical. The class was very sympathetic and supportive; debated the aspects of the ethical challenge and the rationalizations one hears for different actions; and discussed a variety of alternative potential solutions.

As a final independent exercise, students were asked to think about their own experiences again, and to attempt to distill what they felt were their underpinning social values and beliefs that created the personal feelings, drivers, and response they experience in their ethical challenge. Students were then asked to take stock of their level of awareness of their social values in their normal daily working environment. Although majority of students at this stage of the class were quietly reflective, one student expressed a significant level of agitation. When asked if he would like to share his thoughts with the class, the student, who ran his own business, stated that he had never up to this point considered his own personal social values as having a role in his business. Having explored and articulated his social values through the class, he felt he could no longer carry out his business in the same way as he had up to that point, thus causing his agitation, and also significant epiphany in relation to how he might now make his business a better reflection of his own personal social and economic values in the future.

The objective of the class was to provide the MBA students with an introduction to the topic of social entrepreneurship; reflect on the nature of the social mission within social enterprise; and then to reflect on the types of ethical challenges faced in the field, in order to prepare them for their service learning course on social entrepreneurship. Through the application of the GVV for social entrepreneurship teaching case study, the students were able to:

- be introduced to an example of a social entrepreneur and community organization;
- consider the day-to-day challenges faced by social entrepreneurs who manage the balance between commercial realities and social goals;
- give the students an insight into the ethical challenges faced by social entrepreneurs and the mechanisms adopted to stay true to their social mission; avoiding mission drift;
- explore their own values and beliefs;
- reflect on the connection between their own current business practice and their values and beliefs; and
- consider how they might channel their values and beliefs into their own social mission and practice voicing their own values in the future.

Conclusion

While the teaching of social entrepreneurship and the understanding of the specific ethical challenges facing the social entrepreneur is still relatively new, the application of GVV mechanisms within a social entrepreneurship curriculum has illustrated that the practice of voicing of values is vital to the development of the social mission for the social entrepreneur. Through GVV for social entrepreneurship, students are able to explore, identify, and understand their own values and beliefs; convert their values and beliefs into their social mission; and practice voicing their social values in order to stay true to their social goals.

In adopting GVV for social entrepreneurship pedagogy, the following points are pertinent for success:

1. that the GVV curriculum be utilized to allow the student to identify and voice their values and beliefs and then convert these into their social mission for their social enterprise solution; and

2. that through sector-specific case studies depicting the facets of ethical challenges experienced by social entrepreneurs, the students are able to become familiar with, and apply their values to, the creation of responses that will enable them to voice their values when faced with related ethical and moral challenges in the future as social entrepreneurs in practice.

CHAPTER 10

Applying the Giving Voice to Values Framework to Address Leadership Dilemmas

Experiences in an Indian Executive MBA Program

Ranjini Swamy

Abstract

The Indian economy has grown rapidly over the past century and has made steady progress toward integration into the global economy. However, sustained growth and greater integration into the global economy are constrained by governance gaps, as the country struggles to cope with the enhanced complexity in the economic, social, and political spheres. Consequently, the country faces several social and ecological problems such as rising inequality, environmental degradation, and corruption. Given the complexity of these problems, there is a gradual realization that the government, civil society, and business have to work jointly to address them.

This requires new leadership competencies among the leaders of business, government, and civil society. Educational institutions have attempted to inculcate these competencies through courses that have largely focused on imparting conceptual knowledge and skills. There is a need to complement these with courses that promote reflection and action. This chapter describes the author's experience of designing and piloting a course on leadership in an Executive MBA program where the focus was on enabling reflection and (later) action. The GVV framework was introduced to bring participants closer to action. The article shares the session plan and conduct, participants' feedback, and the author's own reflection on the use of GVV framework to help participants appreciate the challenges of leadership.

Keywords

responsible leadership, reflection.

Author Biography

Ranjini Swamy, is Professor of Organization Behavior at Goa Institute of Management, Goa, India. She teaches graduate courses in Organizational Behavior, Training & Development, Leadership and Change Management. She completed her Fellow Programme in Management from Indian Institute of Management, Ahmedabad, India. She has since, been writing cases and articles in the field of social entrepreneurship, Ethics (using the Giving Voice to Values approach) and Corporate Social Responsibility. She has published in the *Human Relations*, *Vikalpa* and *Journal of Business Ethics Education*. She has also presented papers in the Academy of HRD Conference and the Eastern Academy of Management (International) Conference. Some of the cases on Ethics are available on the Giving Voice to Values website.

Applying the GVV Framework to Address Leadership Dilemmas: Experiences in an Executive MBA Program

Background

The Indian economy has grown rapidly over the past century and has made steady progress toward integration into the global economy.[1] However, sustained growth and greater integration into the global economy are constrained by governance gaps, as the country struggles to cope with the enhanced complexity in the economic, social, and political spheres.

Consequently, the country faces several social and ecological problems such as rising inequality,[2] environmental degradation, and corruption.[3] Given the complexity of these problems, there is a gradual realization that the government, civil society, and business have to work jointly to address them. In a recent discussion on building integrity, senior executives in India acknowledged that business could be reinforcing corruption and saw the need to develop a culture of integrity within organizations.[4]

Business enterprises therefore require responsible leadership, that is, a leadership that sees business as a force of social good for many and seeks to achieve a larger social purpose through inclusive and ethical partnerships with all its stakeholders.[5] Such leadership could enhance the legitimacy and sustainability of business over the longer term. For instance, an internet-based survey of 4,000 employees in India found that those rating their organizations low on responsible leadership were four times more likely to leave their organizations than those rating their organizations high on responsible leadership.[6] In a knowledge economy, retention of skilled human resources is critical to sustaining a competitive advantage. To the extent that responsible leadership helps organizations retain their skilled human resources, it enhances business sustainability.

Responsible leaders need to develop enduring, trustful relationships with all their stakeholders, not just with investors.[7] For this, they need to recognize the legitimate claims of *all* stakeholders while making business decisions. They need to dialogue and collaborate with people who are dissimilar, sense and resolve conflicts, and create positive synergy.[8] The older notion of "leader-as-a-boss" does not appear to fit the new role requirements of leaders.

In discharging their new roles, leaders could experience several moral dilemmas, as they have to choose between competing values or priorities. Saraide's chairman Hatim Tyabji presented one such dilemma: The head of one of the largest units of his company was adopting unethical means to achieve (even exceed) the unit's targets. The chairman was committed to being ethical; the question was when to let go of the leader of that unit. If he was let go of immediately, the unit would not meet the quarterly financial targets and the company would not meet its commitment to the Wall Street. If he was retained until the next quarter, employees could infer that being unethical was okay sometimes. The chairman took the painful decision of letting the head of the unit go immediately.[9]

Such choices are more difficult in the face of diverse stakeholders' interests, rapidly changing (and very uncertain) contexts, and increasing business competition. Unless leaders recognize the moral dilemmas in the situation, become clear about their values and priorities, and develop the competencies to resolve the dilemmas ethically,[10] they could compromise the legitimacy of their organizations in the eyes of stakeholders and experience adverse business outcomes.

Approaches to Teaching Leadership

Educational institutions could help inculcate leadership competencies through three types of learning: conceptual, reflective, and action learning.[11] Conceptual learning focuses on helping people understand the concept of leadership and the theories about leadership. Reflective learning focuses on improving self-awareness and insight, which could in turn lead to the development of personally meaningful visions. Action learning provides learners with an opportunity to apply their learning to real-life contexts and thereby internalize some of the leadership skills required.[12]

Typically, courses on leadership in business schools help participants understand the concept of leadership, including responsible leadership. While these are useful, they may not help the students directly link the concepts to their own experiences; therefore, the application and transfer of learning could be inhibited. To overcome this problem, conceptual learning needs to be supplemented by action and reflection. Students could experience leadership situations through simulations; they could then "reflect" on their experiences and draw lessons on leadership. Reflection or "retrospective sense-making," involves looking back at actions and their consequences and making sense of their connection. Reflection becomes necessary as leaders often make decisions in situations where the ends are confusing or conflicting, problems not clearly defined, and outcomes not predictable. Reflection allows leaders to understand their impact on others and the consequences thereof. Such an insight could help leaders think differently about their behaviors, question some of their assumptions, and change them.[13]

Designing the Course on Leadership

Learning Outcomes of the Course

I was preparing to offer an elective on Leadership[14] to participants of an Executive MBA (EMBA) program. Other courses in the program had already provided participants with the conceptual foundations of leadership. I proposed to complement them with a course that promoted reflection on leadership experiences. The question was, "What would leaders need to reflect upon?"

The reading of James March and Thierry Weil's book "On leadership"[15] provided cues about what leaders needed to reflect upon. The book drew on the unpublished lecture notes of Professor James March, which he had used for teaching at the Stanford University. The book provided an up-close, leader-as-mortal look at leadership that resonated with my experiences and with those of many executives whom I taught. It explored several moral and ethical dilemmas facing leaders—for example, balancing the public and private duties—as they discharged their responsibilities. These dilemmas appeared to emerge from the conflicting concerns/expectations of different stakeholders (the self, the in-group, and other stakeholders within or outside the organization). The leader's response to these dilemmas could impact the nature of his relationships with stakeholders and his continued ability to lead. The ideas discussed in this book formed the foundation of my course.

Broadly, the objective of my course was to help participants become aware of some of the leadership dilemmas, examine how different leaders respond to these dilemmas, and explore the consequences of these choices for their ability to establish trustful relationships with stakeholders. In the process, participants could reflect on their responses to similar situations. The resulting insight could help them review their assumptions and behaviors and change them if necessary.

Participant Profile

Participants of the EMBA program had at least 3 years' experience in an executive capacity. They were small entrepreneurs, junior-/middle-level executives in local organizations or academic administrators. The elective on Leadership drew 14 participants out of about 40 participants in the batch; most had more than 5 years of experience as managers or administrators. Of the 14 registered participants, 8 were extremely regular. Discussions during and after the course were thus largely confined to these participants.

Designing for Reflection

Given the objective of the course, a major concern was how to trigger reflection. James March seemed to have achieved this through the discussion of Western literary classics. Could the discussion of Western literary classics enable reflection among the participants of my elective? Like their counterparts elsewhere, executives here had limited time for class preparation. Additionally, in my experience, many participants experienced difficulty in comprehending English and were not inclined to learn through reading. Given their profile, using Western literary classics to promote reflection did not seem appropriate.

I considered the use of films to explore leadership dilemmas and enable reflection. Films could powerfully communicate tacit information about the context and the reactions of stakeholders. In high-context cultures such as in India, communication is more nuanced. What is *not* said often carries more meaning than what is said; again, understanding the meaning of what is said requires understanding the context in which it is said.[16] Given this, films seemed to be a potentially more effective method of promoting reflection about leadership dilemmas. I chose to screen films that were largely Indian, to enhance the contextual relevance.

However, I realized that merely viewing the films would not automatically ensure reflection on the leadership dilemmas. There was need to sensitize participants to the leadership dilemmas *before* they saw the films, so that their attention was directed to the issues of relevance to the course. Accordingly, I decided to use some readings from the book "On Leadership" to prime participants about the leadership dilemmas.[17]

Participants preread an article on a specific leadership dilemma and submitted a summary of the same. The article was then briefly discussed in the class, so that the students could better relate to its content.[18] Participants later viewed a film that depicted a similar dilemma;

postfilm discussions reviewed how the leader in the film had responded to the leadership dilemma, considering why and with what possible consequences for his ability to lead the various stakeholders. Participants were encouraged to share their work-related experiences.

Reflection was more directly promoted through written assignments at the end of the course. In one such assignment, participants were asked to reflect on a leadership dilemma they had experienced, their response to these dilemmas (and rationale for it), and the consequences for their ability to lead the stakeholders. In another assignment, participants were asked to identify and interview a leader they respected. (Many chose to interview a senior executive in their organization.) They described a leadership dilemma faced by the leader, how he responded to it, and the consequences for his ability to lead the stakeholders.

Introducing the GVV Framework

As the course progressed, it appeared from informal feedback that participants experienced greater sensitization to a variety of leadership dilemmas. The junior participants said they began to ask themselves whether they were being effective leaders, and how their actions could affect their stakeholders. The more senior participants were familiar with the leadership dilemmas explored in the sessions. Some realized that the leadership dilemmas applied equally to their personal lives. The films and discussions helped them review their responses to similar dilemmas at their workplace.

However, sensitization to the leadership dilemmas and reflection on their experiences was not sufficient: participants wanted to know how to respond effectively to the leadership dilemmas. They had experienced moral and ethical dilemmas at their workplace but had chosen to remain silent for a variety of reasons. Could there be ways of effectively dealing with such dilemmas? It was in this context that the GVV framework became useful.

Outline of Sessions on GVV

The GVV framework was introduced in the last four sessions of the course to explore ways of effectively enacting one's values in the face of moral and ethical dilemmas. The first two sessions explored the need for moral leadership, the requirements of moral leadership, and the factors facilitating the demonstration of such leadership. The last two sessions presented the GVV framework and helped participants use it to prepare a response to a moral or ethical dilemma.

The First Two Sessions

Participants first preread an article on moral leadership.[19] The session began with a brief presentation about moral leadership and the factors impeding /facilitating its expression in organizations. The viewing of the film, "The Insider," followed this.[20] In the film, Lowell Bergman, the producer of a famous television news-show, had (with great difficulty) persuaded an executive from a tobacco firm to share his views about the addictive potential of cigarettes and what tobacco companies in the United States were doing about it. He felt morally obliged (to the public at large and to his source) to air the interview on his news show. The senior management of his company, however, was not keen on airing this interview on the news show for a variety of business and personal reasons. The film described Lowell's response to the dilemma he faced and the consequences of this for him and for other stakeholders. Participants were asked to view the film and submit a written assignment exploring the moral/ethical dilemma faced by Lowell Bergman, his response to the dilemma and the consequences of his response.

The Last Two Sessions

The GVV framework was presented as an approach available to leaders to effectively enact their strongly held values at the workplace. The crux of the framework was scripting and peer coaching, whereby individuals/ groups developed and strengthened actionable responses to moral dilemmas at the workplace. The framework was applied to the situation facing Lowell Bergman, to demonstrate how it could be used.

In the last session, participants applied the GVV framework to part A of the case-study "The Temple Encroachment issue," which had been distributed earlier. The case described the dilemma faced by a civil servant in India in 2007, when the general assembly elections were due. A reputed Muslim builder had approached the civil servant with a problem: The builder had recently acquired land for commercial development but discovered that the land was being encroached by the neighboring Hindu temple. He wanted the temple authorities to vacate his land and sought the help of the civil servant to make this happen.

After understanding the facts, the civil servant realized that the builder's claims were justified. However, in providing justice to the builder, he risked antagonizing his family members, the local Hindu community who revered the temple and the politician representing the constituency. He also risked compromising the fairness of the election process. Unless the issue was handled sensitively, it could become embarrassing both personally and professionally.

Participants were asked to take on the role of the civil servant and suggest *how* he could enact his values. (Questions derived from the GVV framework served as a guide for developing a script. *See Annexure 1 for the list of questions posed.*) They worked in groups during the class to develop a workable script.

Group Presentation of Their Script

One of the groups was invited to present their script. They first presented the moral dilemma facing the civil servant. They felt he had to choose between (a) being truthful *and* being loyal to the community of which his family was an integral part; (b) appeasing the majority (a short-term solution) *and* providing justice (a longer term solution); and (c) protecting the rights of many *and* protecting the rights of an individual.

The key stakeholders in the situation were the builder, the temple committee/local community, the local politician, the government, the civil servant and his family. Of them, the builder, the temple committee, the government functionaries, and the politician were considered more critical and their stakes were identified. The builder was concerned about realizing the commercial value of his property as soon as possible, the politician about getting re-elected, the government with ensuring fair elections and the community/temple committee about maintaining the religious sanctity of the temple.

Of the key stakeholders, the temple committee and the politician were expected to be most resistant to the civil servant's desire to support the builder's interests. They were likely to interpret the civil servant's desire as pandering to the needs of the minority community. The group developed rational arguments to address the concerns of each of these stakeholders.

Next, the group presented a detailed action plan to persuade the stakeholders to settle the issue justly and amicably: They suggested that the civil servant first meet his higherups and take them into confidence. (The temple issue could potentially compromise the election process; it was therefore better to keep the higherups in the loop.)

The civil servant should then contact the builder and request him to gift the encroached property to the temple. As the builder was rich, influential, and intent on developing the land commercially, this gesture could generate goodwill in the local community and help resolve the issue quickly. (Court proceedings could drag on for long, and impede his ability to develop the land quickly.) However, the group expected that the builder might not be willing to gift the land, given its cost. So the builder would need to be compensated for his loss.

Last, the civil servant could meet the (more receptive) representatives of the temple committee and inform them that (a) they had done something that was not legal; (b) they would need to pay the builder the market price[21] for the encroached land to ensure a more permanent solution to the problem. (The group said different things to the builder and the temple committee to create a space for negotiation later.)

Peer Coaching

Other participants were briefed about the purpose of peer coaching and the role they needed to play. (*See Annexure 2 for details.*) They raised several pertinent points with the presenters: Could there be an ethical solution to such leadership dilemmas? Could the decision made by the civil servant be undone after the elections, when the Election Code was lifted? Would the temple committee members agree to pay the market rate for the encroached land? Even if some representative of the temple committee did agree, would the temple committee endorse his/her decision? Could the civil servant withstand pressures from temple authorities to support them?

Participants were urged to think of ways in which these concerns could be addressed. After a discussion, many participants agreed on the following points:

- an ethical solution was possible because every community had sane and rational-minded people.
- the decision of the civil servant could not be overturned by the politicians later because (a) it was based on the judicial powers delegated to the civil servant during the election process; (b) the stakeholders would have signed a "consent form" agreeing to the solution.

However, there was considerable debate about whether the temple authorities would pay the market rate for the encroached land. Some believed that the temple committee could be willing to pay a more nominal sum (not the market rate) as compensation to the builder.

Participants agreed that an inclusive and ethical solution was possible if all affected stakeholders[22] met and arrived at an agreement through discussion. In the meeting, the civil servant could present the urgency of the situation and request their cooperation to protect the communal harmony in the state. He would need to ensure that emotions did not get out of hand during the discussions. Seeking a legal solution to the problem should occur only later (as a last resort).

Towards the end of the discussion, I shared the gist of the civil servant's response to the leadership dilemma (part B of the case). Participants felt heartened that the civil servant had not compromised on his values. They saw the need for more such examples from leaders in corporate organizations. Some participants related their experiences in similar situations. They suggested that effective enactment of values in response to leadership dilemmas was more likely when executives had strongly developed professional identities.

Observations and Reflections on the Use of GVV Framework

Applying the GVV framework to the case study brought an action-focus into the classroom. It forced participants to explore more effective responses to moral and ethical dilemmas. Participants initially expressed skepticism about whether leadership dilemmas could be resolved ethically. Many had experienced such dilemmas:

> When you work with people for so long, you develop a respect towards the person whom you report to. However when you see the same person asking you to lie or do the things that could harm the company, you find it very difficult ... to respond to such a situation.
>
> (Participant 1)

> Many times it becomes difficult to take a decision on the issues which are ethically wrong but required in company's interest (important for quick and smooth functioning of company). For example, when we have to get materials cleared under "urgency" cases from the Customs, we have to pay ... "express money" i.e., payment for getting work done faster. I'm totally against influencing any one, but being a finance manager in the company, even if I do not want to support or act in such a manner, I'm forced to, as I have to follow my boss's instruction.
>
> (Participant 2)

Some had preferred to change teams (and bosses) or jobs in response to such dilemmas. Others had continued in their jobs, preferring not to confront the boss for a variety of reasons: (a) They did not feel responsible for their actions as they were "forced" to act unethically, (b) they did not want to put their families at risk, or (c) they preferred not to be seen as problem creators. Given this background, they believed that enacting their values at the workplace in response to moral or ethical dilemmas was not practical. Senior administrators among the participants argued that it was possible to address moral and ethical dilemmas effectively. They shared incidents from their experience as supportive evidence.

Participants felt that the use of the GVV framework could help a leader plan his response to moral or ethical dilemmas. As the framework actively addressed stakeholders' concerns, it could reduce the latter's need to manipulate the leader. However, some felt that the GVV approach could not be an "insurance policy against all value conflicts," especially with respect to deeper differences across castes/religions. One respondent described an incident that occurred at her workplace:

Usually the employees at our company sat together to have lunch. Our company had no restriction on what could be eaten. One day, the Catholic employee brought beef for lunch. On seeing her eat beef, the Brahmin employee started yelling about it and asked the Catholic employee to leave the place immediately.

Responding to such value conflicts could be tricky; while the GVV approach could be applied in such situations, it was not clear what to do if the approach failed.

Comments

Given a high-power distance culture, participants need more practice in presenting their values to their superiors in a way that does not generate negative feelings. They also need exposure to role models who manage to do this effectively. There is a need to develop case studies or simulations that address this issue.

Could the GVV approach help address value conflicts between members of different religious communities, especially those with a history of conflict? This issue is important because caste- or religious-diversity at the workplace is set to increase in India. To resolve such valueconflicts, leaders need to decide their priorities. (The GVV approach assumes that the leader knows what values he would like to voice and then helps him/her voice these values more effectively.) Also, all stakeholders need to agree to (a) play down the communal angle (b) respect the law and (c) go by evidence. In other words, a strongly developed professional (acquired) identity could be essential.

Future Plans

Applying the GVV framework allowed participants to get actively involved in helping a leader behave ethically. Developing a script and presenting it to peers helped address skepticism and link participants' experiences to classroom learning. I expect to integrate the GVV approach more fully into the course, so that participants get more practice in addressing leadership dilemmas and more actively link their experiences to classroom learning.

This requires developing appropriate learning materials (cases, movies, and video-discussions) that meet the following objectives:

- demonstrate that leadership dilemmas faced in hierarchical societies can be inclusively and ethically addressed;
- demonstrate that leaders *can choose to* respond ethically and inclusively to such dilemmas and the outcomes of such choices are not always unfavorable;
- provide opportunities to script and coach peers, so that existing assumptions and feelings associated with enacting values can be examined and tested.

It may be useful to extend the classroom learning to the workplace through the EMBA participants' Work-Improvement-Project. This project is implemented during the last (third) year of the EMBA program at our Institute. It offers participants an opportunity to apply what is learnt during the program and thereby improve their workplace in significant ways. Interested participants in this course could take up a project to address leadership dilemmas they face at their workplace. They could practice using the GVV framework to obtain the cooperation and trust of the stakeholders as they work toward realizing their objectives.

Glossary

Responsible leadership: Leadership that sees business as a force of social good for many and seeks to achieve a larger social purpose through inclusive and ethical partnerships with all its stakeholders.

Reflection: Retrospective sense-making, that is, looking back at actions and their consequences and making sense of their connection.

Annexure 1

Scripting a Response to Moral Dilemma

- What are the values at stake for the decision maker?
- Who are the people who would be affected by the decision?

- What is at stake for them?
- What arguments could they have against the voicing of the decision maker's values?
- What could be the most powerful response against each argument?
- Whom would you approach? In what order?
- Will you approach the person alone/in company with some others?
- How would you frame the issue?
- What levers would you use to persuade them?
- What role would you adopt?
- When/where would you approach them?

Annexure 2

Peer Coaching

For Listeners

You need to adopt the role of joint problem solvers. You are on the same side of the fence as the presenter. Assume you are the target audience of presenters and answer the following:

- What would your reactions be?
- What are the strengths of the plan presented?
- What issues still need to be addressed?
- How could the plan be strengthened?

For Presenters

- What were the strengths of your presentation?
- What are some of the concerns which you think need addressing?
- Did you find the feedback helpful? Why?
- How do you intend to respond?

CHAPTER 11

Giving Voice to Values in Operations Management

Kathleen E. McKone-Sweet

Abstract

This chapter discusses the importance of values-driven leadership for operations management and presents the use of a *Giving Voice to Values* (GVV) case for teaching sustainability and supply chain management. We briefly summarize the *Filipe Montez* case, describe how this case is positioned within a supply chain management (SCM) course and how the case relates to other SCM topics, and present a teaching approach for the case. We also discuss the benefits to students and faculty by using GVV cases in operations management courses.

Keywords

operations management, supply chain, sustainability, pedagogy.

Author Biography

Kate McKone-Sweet is professor of Operations Management and chair of the Technology, Operations, and Information Management Division at Babson College. Her teaching and research focus on supply chain management. McKone-Sweet is also the coauthor of the book, *The New Entrepreneurial Leader: Developing Leaders Who Shape Social and Economic Opportunity* (September 2011). The book embraces a three-principle model for reinventing management education and provides examples of how educators across all disciplines are integrating these ideas into their courses. McKone-Sweet is also in the process of developing a new *Giving Voice to Values* case for use in her supply chain management course.

GVV in Operations Management

In recent years, my colleagues and I have introduced more cases and discussions about social and environmental sustainability in our operations management courses. We are often surprised by the responses. Some students are excited and engaged by the discussion while others ask "How does this relate to operations management—this seems more like an ethics discussion?" It amazes us that so many students, and managers for that matter, still do not understand that ethics and sustainability are not separate from how we do business and how we operate the firm. These types of comments motivate me to modify and improve the quality of sustainability and ethics discussions in my operations management courses.

It is important for students to understand that shared value creation and operations management decisions are closely linked but are not necessarily easy to carry out. There are inherent tensions among social, environmental, and economic value creation. Therefore, an operations manager must become adept at engaging many stakeholders in the process of creating new solutions to traditional operations management problems. They must become skilled at shaping implementation plans that enable them to engage those within their organizations and to partner with external stakeholders. It is important, therefore, for operation management educators to provide students with the skills and experiences to tackle these tough problems. The GVV teaching approach can support faculty in their efforts to engage students in implementing operations management plans that shape social and economic value.

This chapter will focus on the use of the GVV operations management case called "*This Whole System Seems Wrong*": *Felipe Montez and Concerns about the Global Supply Chain*[1] (referred to as the *Felipe Montez* case). We will briefly summarize the *Filipe Montez* case, describe how this case is positioned within a supply chain management (SCM) course and how the case relates to other SCM topics, and present a teaching approach for the case. We hope to show the importance of the GVV approach to students learning operations management.

GVV Case Example

The *Felipe Montez* case[2] is a wonderful GVV case for either a core operations management or a supply chain management course. It helps students consider issues of social responsibility and supplier management as well as the challenges of managing a global supply chain. Most importantly, it asks students to develop a script and experiment with taking responsibility for and implementing sustainability initiatives.

The case presents a situation in which Felipe Montez was hired to be a purchasing director and product designer for a Spanish electronics company. The company has a 27-year history of working with a Hong Kong distributor. Felipe's new responsibilities will now involve directly managing the supplier relationships in order to reduce the distributor's mark-ups. On Felipe's first trip to China, he visited several factories and found a wide range of conditions. He was most concerned about the conditions (which included child workers and unsafe working conditions) in the factory that produced the majority of his company's goods. When he returned from China, he spoke with his manager who largely dismissed the issues and expressed concerns over cost management. After reviewing other industry practices, Felipe decided that he would like the company to make changes in the management of suppliers. However, as a junior member of the staff, Felipe is concerned that he could undermine his credibility in the company and wonders what steps he should take next.

This three-page case places students in the role of Felipe and presents a rich example for class discussion. It helps to prepare students for their future roles as operations managers by (a) exposing them to social sustainability issues, (b) allowing them to develop a script and, through role playing, practice presenting their argument, and (c) deepen the discussions of other supply chain topics.

Fit of Case within SCM Course

This case is positioned in the last third of a supply chain course in a module on Corporate Sustainability. This module explores the complexity of creating social and economic value and highlights how supply chain decisions can positively or negatively affect social and environmental outcomes.

The module begins with the case, *Wal-Mart Sustainability Strategy*,[3] which describes Wal-Mart's corporate environmental sustainability program and the progress made by three industry groups within the company. The students are asked to assess the sustainability program and to determine which industry group was most successful, what factors made their approach successful and whether or not the approach could be applied to other industry groups. This introductory class presents an example of sustainability initiatives at a large organization. To supplement the case, we also discuss some of Wal-Mart's failures related to social sustainability—labor conditions, discrimination cases, and so forth—and discover how the company's low cost, lean approach may lead to difficult working conditions both within Wal-Mart and for suppliers. This class discussion highlights the tensions from balancing social, environmental, and economic value creation.

For the next class session, students review four Corporate Sustainability reports rated as leading reports by the Global Reporting Initiative. A group of students is tasked with assessing each report. Students identify the strengths and weakness of each report including the presence or absence of relevant information, the metrics for assessment, and the progress made by the company. The students also compare the content of the reports to the available press reports on the company. During the class, the students generate a list of best practices for measuring, delivering, and tracking sustainability performance and emphasize the need for better consistency across sustainability reports.

The third class in the module is focused on social sustainability issues and utilizes the *Felipe Montez* case for discussion. The goals for this class include (a) exposing students to social sustainability issues, (b) connecting students to the role that they may soon play in a company's sustainability efforts, and (c) allowing students to develop action plans and create scripts that will enable them to practice the implementation of these action plans. The case also connects well to other SCM topics covered in the course, including outsourcing, partner selection, and global challenges.

Outsourcing

Prior to the sustainability module, we discuss the benefits and risks of outsourcing. Clearly, outsourcing can lead to cost and volume flexibility advantages and can allow a company to focus on its core competencies. There are numerous examples, such as Nike, Apple, and Cisco, where a company has outsourced production in order to focus on their marketing and research and development efforts. What is often overlooked in these earlier discussions is the complexity of managing outsourcing relationships. The *Felipe Montez* case helps to highlight some risks and challenges of managing these relationships and opens up the discussion to include supplier codes of conduct, supplier auditing procedures, and a firm's accountability for outsourcing practices.

Partner Selection

When we discuss partner selection earlier in the course, we consider the importance of the alignment of each partner's objectives, the resources, and competencies of each partner, and the structure of service-level agreements. The *Felipe Montez* case allows us to refer back to these discussions and to emphasize the need for clear expectations between partners and regular check-ins on performance. The case also provides an opportunity to discuss the role that distributors or other in-country partners may play in managing suppliers.

Global Challenges

In this course, we also discuss numerous global challenges: fluctuating exchange rates, flexibility/efficiency trade-offs, longer lead times, customs procedures and delays, and cultural differences. This case allows us to consider the reputational risks associated with the performance and practices of global suppliers and manufacturers.

The *Felipe Montez* GVV case discussion provides the opportunity to expand on past class discussions, discuss social and economic sustainability, and engage students in taking action.

Teaching Approach[4]

In preparation for this class, the students read the case and prepare the following study questions.

- What are the main arguments that you are trying to counter?

- Who are the different stakeholders, including those who disagree with you? What is at stake for each of them?
- What levers can be used to influence those with whom you disagree?
- What is the best response to the situation? Who might you engage as allies?
- Who should you talk with first?

The students are also asked to develop a script for the argument that they will make to Felipe's manager. This prework helps students to understand the complexity of the situation faced by Felipe and to spend time developing an action plan for Felipe. An on-line preparation approach for students is also described in Appendix A.

A sample timeline for class activities and discussions is shown in Exhibit 11.1. Obviously, the times can be adjusted for different class lengths and audiences. Students arrive to the classroom and find a slide show projecting photos taken from similar Chinese factories. This sets the tone for the class by helping students to visualize the factory conditions Felipe may have seen when visiting China.

Exhibit 11.1. Class Timeline

Class timing	Activity	Activity topics
10 minutes	Discuss	Issues at play and different perspectives
5 minutes	Discuss	Stakeholders and what is at stake
10 minutes	Practice (one on one)	Student share scripts and provide feedback
20 minutes	Discuss	Possible action plans and potential arguments Possible levers of influence
10 minutes	Practice (group)	Student 1 presents to class and is given feedback
10 minutes	Practice (group)	Student 2 presents to class and is given feedback
5 minutes	Discuss	Wrap up of case
15 minutes	Short lecture	Wrap up of sustainability module
85 minutes	Total	

As the class discussion begins, students are asked about the different issues that are at play in the case situation. Typically, students respond from the perspective of Felipe and discuss how he must be balancing his desire to act on his values with his desire to be a respected employee in his new role. Others discuss the long term effect that his actions might have on his career. It is fun to challenge the students on whether or not it is okay to wait to act on their values until they are in a leadership position and if they do so, if their values will be the same after years of denying them in their early career roles.

The class discussion continues to explore other perspectives and their associated problems or obstacles. From the manager's perspective, students talk about his responsibility for supply chain efficiency and maintaining low costs. Others may take the perspective of the Chinese factory managers and discuss the cost pressures they experience from customers and their role in supporting the economic development of China. Finally, students may also bring up personal viewpoints that support or combat globalization. This discussion leads to the identification of the key stakeholders and the potential risks and benefits for each.

After this introductory discussion, students are asked to break into teams of two for 10 minutes and to share and provide feedback on their actions plans. This peer-to-peer exercise allows the students to share their plans and provide feedback in a nonthreatening atmosphere. As the students come back to the large group, they present the possible short- and long-term action plans for Felipe and then highlight the arguments that he may encounter with specific actions. Finally, plans are refined as we discuss the key levers that can be used to influence others. Sample action plans, arguments, and levers are presented in Exhibit 11.2.

Students often take different approaches to developing their scripts and arguments. However, the strongest responses

- address both short-term and long-term economic effects of taking or not taking action;
- identify both short-term fixes and long-term modifications to the way that they handle their suppliers;

Exhibit 11.2. Actions Plans and Arguments

Timing	Sample of student responses
Short term Actions for Felipe	• Talk to factory managers about concerns and raise awareness of other practices • Provide quick fixes such as magnifying glasses to improve factory work • Ask for work time to focus on long-term fixes
Long-term Actions for Felipe	• Establish supplier code of conduct and conduct regular audits • Look into labor laws and encourage compliance • Work internally on planning processes to balance work load • Look for and use resources from industry groups • Seek out mentors within the company
Possible Arguments	• Negative impact on short-term profits • Negative impact on ability to compete in industry • Small changes won't make a real difference • The system works this way; we can't change this • Factories won't invest in this and they may drop us as client • Current system provides jobs and workers choose to work here • Inability to enforce new code of conduct
Possible Levers	• Protect company/brand reputation • Maintain legal and regulatory standards • Increase productivity through improved labor conditions • Have charitable arm of company support improvements in the factories • Ensure cost of fixes would not be more than cost reduction associated with Felipe's oversight of suppliers • Provide easy and feasible ways of doing the right thing • Consider negative outcomes from unsafe working condition—are paints okay for product safety and so forth

- engage the manager as a potential collaborator rather than an adversary—assume that the manager would be willing to make changes if an economic case can be made for taking action;
- recognize that there are a number of levers that can be used to influence the manager and others in the company: brand reputation, legal and regulatory standards, productivity benefits, and potential cost reductions in the long term;
- consider how the company's charitable arm may be able to focus more directly on opportunities within their own supply chain;
- utilize examples to support the argument: Failures or successes of other companies, the role of the UN Global Compact and

the policies and practices from industry groups such as the Electronic Industry Citizenship Coalition.

Once the possible action plans have been discussed, one student is asked to present her script (either in its original form or a revised form that incorporates the ideas from the class discussions). After presenting the script, the student shares how she felt when placed in Filipe's role and what she would change if she were able to do it over. The discussion is then opened to the class, and all students have an opportunity to offer suggestions for improvement. Next, the class is asked if anyone has a different approach from the first. A second student is then asked to present the script that he has developed. The presenter and the other students are both given an opportunity to provide feedback in a similar manner.

After these two practice sessions, the students are asked about the key lessons from the case and the exercise. Additional comments can be added by the faculty member to bring the discussion to its conclusions. The remaining class time is used to present some best practices of supplier codes of conduct and examples of industry-wide initiatives that have tried to change the game of off-shore production.

This teaching approach has been effective at highlighting the types of social sustainability issues that an operations manager may experience early in his career. It also provides students an opportunity to learn how to address the concerns of various stakeholders, develop an action plan, and engage others in support of their plan. This experience helps prepare students for action when they are faced with similar sustainability issues in the future.

Benefits of GVV for Operations Management

There are a number of benefits from using this GVV case and teaching approach in SCM or other operations management courses. From a faculty perspective, the case provides a short case that enables students to understand the complexity of social sustainability issues and how operations management decisions affect social and economic value creation. It also provides an easy approach for bringing ethics into the operations management discussion. Faculty can feel comfortable assessing the students' action plans using their strong background and experience with operation management.

From the student perspective, this unique experiential learning experience helps to break up the monotony of standard case discussions. It offers a different way for the students to prepare for and participate in class. Through the GVV exercises, students practice solving a problem, creating a solution, and taking action to develop their knowledge of social sustainability and their skills at giving voice to their values.

The GVV case also allows students to apply the operations concepts and language from the course and expand their perceptions of the role of operations management. The GVV cases help demonstrate that operations management is not simply about analysis and problem solving but also involves ethics and corporate sustainability and responsibility.

Appendix A: An On-Line Supplement to the Case

The on-line model assigns students to groups of four to five students. Each group has its own on-line discussion area where it has 3 days to respond to the assignment questions and consider the best approach of action for Filipe. Then one group member is asked to make a video as they present their action plan and try to gain support from their manager. The other team members review the presentation and provide feedback on how the script (its clarity and persuasiveness) and the student's delivery (tone, body language) could be improved. Once the faculty member reviews the discussions and videos, two groups are asked to post videos of their revised approach.

During the on-line preparation, the faculty member can review the discussions and ask questions that might help the students to develop a deeper understanding of the issues or to develop a more persuasive argument. Also, a review of videos provides an opportunity to learn about the different approaches taken by the teams. There are several benefits of this approach: Quieter students often feel more comfortable contributing in the on-line discussion format; students frequently use more on-line resources to learn more about supplier codes of conduct and industry practices; students work in teams to analyze the situation and develop a script ahead of time (providing more time for in-class discussion); and the faculty member has the opportunity to see the differences and similarities of the team approaches and can use this knowledge to broaden the in-class discussion.

Given this prework, the in-class schedule can be adjusted, shortening the discussion time, and lengthening the time for practice and role-playing. It also provides more time to discuss the pros and cons of specific approaches and how one approach might fit better with one's personal style and approach. The in-class time can also include additional role-playing. For example, a new role-play, where the faculty plays the manager and the student plays Felipe, can provide an experience where students not only deliver their script but also respond to a variety of arguments from the manager.

CHAPTER 12

Voicing Values in Marketing Education

Indian Perspectives

Subhasis Ray

Abstract

Management education in emerging markets such as India faces the challenge of preparing future business managers who are ethically grounded and are able to compete with their global peers. Curriculums in most of the 3000+ business schools lack components dealing with ethics, corporate governance, and corporate social responsibility. While many students aspire for roles in sales and marketing, marketing management education is conspicuous by the absence of topics related to marketing ethics and values. This chapter narrates the effort and learning in introducing the Giving Voi᷈ to Values (GVV) approach in courses related to marketing ᷈ t, sales and distribution management, and business-to-᷈ g in a leading Indian B-school. GVV's practice-based ᷈ handling ethical dilemmas was found useful by mar-᷈ s courses. India needs wider faculty adoption and ᷈ to reinforce the possibility of voicing values suc-᷈ ᷈ging business environment.

Keywords

Author Biography

Subhasis Ray is Associate Professor in Xavier Institute of Management Bhubaneswar (XIMB), India. He teaches courses related to marketing, sustainability, and corporate social responsibility. His research interest is at the intersection of sustainability and marketing. (mail.sray@gmail.com)

Values in Indian Management Education

Values and primacy of value-based education have featured in Indian thought and writing for more than 5000 years in its scriptures and epics, starting with the Vedas (ancient Indian scriptures). Ethics of governance and business formed the basis of the classic text *"Artha Shastra"* (The Treatise on Money) written by Chanakya, arguably India's most famous diplomat-economist-politician who lived in the 3rd century BC. More recently, during the British occupation of India, Gandhi's view that business is the custodian of society's wealth shaped the worldview of leading Indian industrialists such as Jamnalal Bajaj and GD Birla. The value-driven business orientation of the Tata group is also well known.

Modern Indian management education started about 60 years back but flourished in the mid-1990s with the liberalization of the Indian economy. This created the need for a large number of managers trained in the ways of managing growing corporations. As of August 2012, more than 3,500 business schools produced about 352,350 managers in India.[1] In relation to values-driven education, the picture is dismal. In a national workshop conduced at the Indian Institute of Management, Bangalore, on ethics, corporate governance, and corporate social responsibility,[2] it was found that less than 100 business schools, covered these subjects as per the information their website or response to survey questions. Even if we adjust for the sample size, response rate, and lack of web presence of school curriculum, the number is too low for anybody's comfort. The need for value-driven management education, by contrast, becomes clearer when one looks at the major business scandals that rocked India in telecom, mining, and other sectors in 2011–2012. Involvement large industrial houses in corruption-related issues and the lack tical approaches in handling ethical dilemmas have hea credibility of business ethics and marketing teaching in Indian business schools. For example, in industrial marketing, all-pervasive corruption has become endemic.[3] I fear that this situation will worsen unless targeted interventions are planned in the curriculum of Indian business schools.

Though the issue of values is very relevant across Indian business education, this chapter focuses on the Giving Voice to Values (GVV) approach to address value-related issues in marketing management. Ethics and compliance officers from the world's largest companies have identified sales and doing business in emerging markets as their top two areas of greatest concern in relation to building ethical culture in their organizations.[4] From our experience, most MBA-level jobs in India are in sales and marketing, including customer facing roles in the financial sector and the IT. However, as discussed earlier, content-related marketing ethics and values are conspicuous by their absence from Indian B-school curriculum. The institutions are creating a large number of marketing managers who do not have any grounding in ethics and are ill-equipped to handle ethical dilemmas in the workplace. Hence, there is a need to address this gap as well as the cynicism from the students about the role of ethical behavior in sales and marketing. GVV addresses this need well. In the following sections, I describe the effort to bring GVV into marketing courses and the lessons learned in one of the top-ranked business schools in India.

Ethics in Marketing Courses and the GVV Approach

Marketing educators try to bring values conflicts and their resolution mechanisms into the classroom through pedagogical innovations, such as case studies, role-plays, and movies. Since most case studies used in Indian business schools are based on Western businesses, Indian students find it difficult to relate to them. Role plays and movies being fictional do not always reflect the multidimensional sales and marketing problems in the field. There are very few teaching resources for Indian educators that address the ethical issues in marketing. One of the most popular text books for core marketing courses[5] does not reflect the ethical crisis in Indian markets, leaving it to individual institutions and faculty to decide their focus. In electives such as Sales and Distribution Management (SDM), which I teach, there is an urgent requirement to reinforce the ethical fiber of the trade. Managing sales teams and marketing channels involve a number of ethical issues. Here again, popular textbooks by Indian authors are silent on the almost daily dilemmas faced by sales managers and executives across companies. The same can be said about another popular elective in Indian B-schools: Business to Business (B2B) Marketing. Both these electives stress the field-based application of principles. Faculty members teaching these subjects in executive education programs often face experienced students who share how the practice is corrupt and how difficult it is to handle or change such practices.

While business ethics is taught in some Indian business schools (it's an elective course in many and does not exist in most), it is generally offered as a stand-alone course, focusing more on the philosophical and moral underpinnings of ethical decision making. Students generally do not have any exposure to the topic of how to stand by their ethics and value systems when faced with a problem in the workplace. In marketing ethics, relevant topics relate to product, price, place, and promotion (the 4-Ps of marketing). Ethical issues in marketing range from the authenticity of the market research process, decisions on product quality, and the accuracy of marketing communications. Although sometimes such issues are covered in marketing courses as well as ethics classes, such discussions tend to vary across courses and years.

The focus of the existing ethics-related discussion in marketing courses is often on the corporation as opposed to the individual managers. In application-based courses such as B2B marketing and sales and distribution management, ethical decisions are involved at three broad levels: the corporations' stance on offering the right mix of the 4-Ps and its policies and processes; the managers' decision to pursue a deal ethically and close it without compromising stakeholder values; and finally, the frontline sales person's ability to tackle ethical dilemmas. Though these three levels are based on organizational hierarchy, in each of them, it is the individual's decision that plays a major role in subsequent events. For example, the general manager's insistence to win deals at any cost often sets the ball rolling along a corruption-ridden path. Conventional case studies present a conflict situation highlighting the dilemmas, often leaving the students wondering whether it is practically feasible to voice their values to colleagues and customers, without putting their job at risk.

GVV finds a niche for marketing educators in the current setting. It provides practical case studies of dilemmas. It also shows how executives have faced ethical conflicts—*successfully*. The positive ending is particularly important to reinforce that value dilemmas could be handled successfully and corruption and unethical practices are not the bedrocks of businesses, particularly in the context of emerging economies. Though I use live examples of organizations like Infosys and movies like "Rocket Singh— Salesman of the year," they do not exercise the students' mind on the possibilities in the same way as an issue-driven GVV case. The cases score because they answer the "how to speak out" question rather than "what to speak" question. Having worked in the sales and marketing function in large multinationals, I have personally felt that most values conflicts are not large and larger conflicts provide more defined positions to take. For example, in the case of bribing, one can take a position to bribe or not to bribe. But conflicts in the daily life of marketing managers are more innocuous ones, for example, those involving suppressing information, playing along with dominant wrong doers, or giving wrong or incomplete information to a customer. This experience motivated me to take up GVV as a way to counter the hardening minds of young managers. The biggest reason for taking up GVV rather than conventional case studies from business schools was the fact that they are based on real-life experiences of executives and the methods suggested for voicing values are based on academic rigor. As we discuss later, this logic was helpful in using GVV in executive education.

GVV in Indian Marketing Management Education

I used GVV case studies in four courses—Sales and Distribution Management (SDM—an elective course), Marketing Management II (a core course in marketing), B2B Marketing, and Stakeholder Marketing. The last one is an innovative course that integrates corporate social responsibility, sustainability, and stakeholder orientation within the marketing framework. For all the courses, students were asked to reflect on their own life experience, using the "Tale of Two Stories" format. They were asked to think of two situations where they did and did not act according to their value systems. After this warm-up and initial reflections, the GVV cases were discussed.

The GVV cases were first discussed within a course on Stakeholder Marketing (2011). The GVV case "The Temple Encroachment Issue" (A & B) was discussed. In this case, the protagonist is a young bureaucrat who had to resolve conflict between a Muslim builder and the management of a Hindu temple at a politically volatile time. The builder complained that the temple authorities were illegally encroaching on his land. The conflict had the potential to escalate into a community clash. The case was highly relevant as such conflicts are common in many parts of India. During the discussion, it was helpful to have a student in the class who was a bureaucrat himself. The case was not a traditional ethical marketing case focusing on business and product-related dilemmas. Rather, in line with the course orientation, it was positioned with twin objectives: (a) how industrial projects get embroiled in sensitive local issues, and (b) how solutions could be found and *marketed* with the help of stakeholders. The protagonist noted the help he received from his colleagues, friends, families, superiors, as well as the conflicting parties.

Students appreciated the steps taken by the protagonist. His effort to understand the issue in detail before acting (e.g., legal implication of acting/not acting), finding allies among stakeholders (superiors and temple committee members), and working with the aggrieved parties ensured that he could successfully convince the temple authorities to dismantle their illegal construction and make the builder pay part of the losses that the temple authority incurred. After the case was discussed, students, who were earlier skeptical about voicing values, agreed that it is indeed possible to do so in such sensitive situations. They could realize that such dilemmas *can* always be addressed even if not fully resolved. This differentiation was specifically mentioned by them in the postcourse feedback.

The second instance where GVV was discussed was in introductory marketing courses for working executives. The case on "Product Safety and Preemptive Recall" was discussed to highlight the ethical issues marketing executives faced. The case revolves around an infant nutritional supplement. Company-sponsored market research found that adults also found the product useful as part of their detoxification routine. The company's marketing department wanted to highlight this benefit. The protagonist, however, found some unpublished studies on the Internet that related reduced effectiveness to flu shots with adults who had used the supplement. She had the option of calling off the marketing campaign but that could jeopardize her career in the company. The case led to a lively discussion as many students could relate to the dilemma. While discussing the possible arguments that the protagonist could use, many students agreed on the idea that the company conducted a workshop with leading scientists who could bring more clarity to the issue. This was sort of a mid-way approach that did not force them to take a final decision.

The GVV case "B*e careful what you wish for"* was discussed in a sales and distribution course (2012) to highlight the ethical dilemmas in relation to sales and other functions within an organization. The average work experience of participants was 2 years. The case is about Sarah, who has recently moved to the accounting department after being in the sales department. The company has received a large order but the customer has asked for a delayed delivery. Sarah is asked to bill the order but keep the consignment in the warehouse, so that the sales team can meet its target and get the bonus. This is indeed a very common issue for executives managing marketing channels. Meeting monthly or quarterly targets often creates pressure to take unethical decisions related to billing or dumping of products in collusion with customers or channel members. Many students could identify similar cases they faced during their internships with leading companies.

Interestingly, I wanted to use a case that was not about corruption or bribery—a common issue in Indian business settings and where a clear stand may be more obvious, if not necessarily easy to adopt. Rather, the case selected was about a relatively softer issue, a "small thing" (as described by a participant) that is almost commonplace in managerial life and could be overlooked.

Three role-plays were done before the case discussion. In each role-play, one student played the role of the boss and the other played the role of the protagonist, Sarah. The volunteers playing Sarah's role discussed the dilemma in front of their "boss." After the role-play, the discussion started.

Although the role-plays helped to quickly surface some of the popular counterarguments in voicing values (e.g., fudging information is a common practice or the fact that timing of billing is not really relevant as long as the order is in hand), traditional role-plays are not the approach most suited to the GVV pedagogy. A more scripted approach, where students are asked to prepare a script that spells out Sarah's values and a feasible solution, will work better rather than the random dynamics of a role-play. Following role-play, the discussion centered on the costs involved for all stakeholders and the possible levers that the executive can use. Most students agreed on the importance of researching and reflecting on the situation in advance and developing allies on such occasions. This discussion, held during the last class of the Sales and Distribution course, reinforced the possibility of ethical decision making.

The same case was also repeated in a smaller batch size of 15 experienced executives in a course on B2B marketing with limited success. Participants, who were experienced managers, wondered how often one can voice their values in the current business environment. However, when they were asked to reflect on the purpose of their work, some of them appreciated the fact that giving voice to values is important when one considers the broad purpose of life and living. The usual cynicism for marketing ethics was to some extent countered when they were told that GVV cases are based on real-life incidents and most of them are positive stories.

Findings

Before discussing course-specific learning, I want to mention some common findings. Most students were critical of the GVV idea when it was introduced. After discussing the cases, we found, a significant change in the classroom mood. In all the courses, where GVV was used, about 20 to 30 percent of the students have faced a nonwork situation where they have struggled in articulating their values. More interestingly, only a few of them realized (before the class) that the problem was one of communication.

The students in the core marketing course were fresh out of their engineering colleges. The inexperienced students came to understand that value dilemmas exist in many seemingly mundane marketing jobs like collecting data during marketing research and that they could work to develop the possibility of handling such dilemmas successfully without leaving their job. The fact that they could have a choice was appreciated by most students.

The GVV cases were more successful with students who had some prior work experience. Many of them came from large Indian IT companies such as Infosys, Wipro, TCS, and so forth, where they have either experienced or seen cases of ethical conflict. It was a huge realization for them that value-based decisions are not binary in nature and many of them commented that this could be very helpful in handling such issues in future. Of particular interest to them was the possibility of articulating their values in a conflict situation.

For both groups of students, we found a significant number of skeptics at the beginning of the discussion. When we used a simple voting system, before and after the case discussion, we could see that many of the early critics were converted after the discussion. More than the faculty, this was a powerful experience for the minority students who believed in voicing values in the first place.

Students in our executive education courses are middle managers having five to seven years of work experience. As reported earlier, GVV met with limited success with this group as they were cynical about its possibilities. In future, more than one case, preferably set in India, could be discussed, to show the possibilities of GVV in different areas. Another approach could be to start with an introductory video that explained the research and rationale behind GVV, followed by a discussion, and then to introduce the case. This could help the faculty to create common grounds for fruitful discussion. A third approach could be to use GVV with other teaching materials like movie clippings and then compare and contrast the learning from them.

Though GVV cases generated fair amount of enthusiasm among students, none of the students came forward to contribute their own life stories. Given the size of India's business sector and the scale of the scams that were unfolding in the late 2012, India needs many more GVV-style cases to drive home the possibility of value-driven business leadership.

Another challenge for GVV in the Indian context is its positioning within the business school curriculum. Student enrollment in courses is determined by their perceived relevance for potential recruiters. Hence, putting GVV as a stand-alone course risks nonsubscription. A possible option—one that is entirely in alignment with the GVV curriculum objectives and the option I selected—is to integrate the cases across functions (e.g., in marketing, HR, and finance). The GVV case collection offers helpful guidance for selecting cases that will be appropriate to different courses.

Beyond the concept itself and its cases, GVV's achievement is to bring ethics out of the Business Ethics curriculum. For the next step, it requires adoption and acceptance of the case method as well as wider dissemination of the concept. A core group of faculty in a region can achieve this purpose, possibly through cobranded GVV-based courses and the development of region-specific case collections. Indeed a new initiative is currently underway, in partnership with the United Nations Global Compact's Principles for Responsible Management Education, to develop a suite of India-based GVV cases. Overall, the concept of GVV requires wider and more frequent articulation through workshops and case studies.

Conclusion

GVV addresses the crying need for value-based business leadership in emerging economies such as India. The cases fill a gap in the current curriculum and help the business school marketing faculty handle ethics and values issues with more confidence. The students see the possibilities related to a career that does not automatically call for a compromise or conflict in decision making but a safe middle ground that can be crafted using proven techniques. Business schools can use the approach to instill ethical decision making among students as well as a marker for their commitment to build a values-driven, new generation of managers. Going forward, Indian business organizations will also find it useful for executive training, given the increasing focus and new regulations in the area of corporate governance. Wider use of GVV will be important to empower Indian business, business schools, and all related stakeholders, given India's possibility to be one of the top three global economic superpowers by 2030.

CHAPTER 13

Giving Voice to Values and Ethics Across the Curriculum at the United States Air Force Academy[1]

Claudia J. Ferrante,
Patrick E. Heflin, and David A. Levy

Abstract

The United States Air Force Academy is an institution committed to developing leaders of character. Intrigued by its potential, the authors brought aspects of the Giving Voice to Values program into its core management course. This chapter reports on their initial experience and suggests that the program may add significant value even to institutions that already provide substantial ethics and values training.

Keywords

Giving Voice to Values, United States Air Force Academy, ethics, training.

Author Biography

Dr. Claudia J. Ferrante is professor of Management and director of Strategic Curriculum for Management in the Department of Management at the United States Air Force Academy. Her research focuses on the application of organizational behavior theory to human capital in the workplace, ethical decision making, and volunteerism as a mechanism for corporate social responsibility. Dr. Ferrante's publications include articles in *Human Resource Management, Trends in Organizational Behavior, Journal of Management Education, Journal of Engineering and Technology Management, Group and Organization Management, International Human Resource Information Management, Business Horizons, Journal of Academic Ethics,* and the *Journal of Management Policy and Practice.*

Lieutenant Colonel Patrick Heflin, PhD, is assistant professor of Management in the Department of Management at the United States Air Force Academy. His research focuses primarily on the effects of organizational structure and control on individual behavior, using Social Identity Theory and Psychological Reactance Theory, among others. He teaches the core Management and Command course as well as classes in the domains of Organizational Theory and Organizational Behavior.

David Levy is professor of Management at the United States Air Force Academy. His current research involves developing cognitive maps of effective leadership. Dr. Levy is the coauthor of *The 52nd Floor, Attitudes Aren't Free,* and *Echoes of Mind.*

In the Fall of 2011, one of the authors of this chapter received an e-mail from a member of the United States Air Force Academy's Center for Character and Leadership Development. The e-mail was a request for United States Air Force Academy (USAFA) faculty members to pair up with distinguished faculty from other institutions during an upcoming National Character and Leadership Symposium hosted by USAFA. The author was asked to pair up with Mary Gentile, the creator of the *Giving Voice to Values* curriculum. Since USAFA understands the importance of values-driven leadership, has ethics training deeply embedded into its curriculum in multiple areas based on its foundational core value of integrity, and even has its own center for character and leadership development, the author was a bit skeptical about what value this pairing could bring. It turns out that the pairing was fortuitous in that the GVV program provides an important addition to USAFA's curriculum. The following chapter provides insight into the uniqueness of the military environment, the importance of values-driven leadership, and how the USAFA uses GVV to enhance its curriculum and meet its mission, "To educate, train and inspire men and women to become leaders of character, motivated to lead the United States Air Force in service to our nation."

Military Environment and the Importance of Values-Driven Leadership

Most organizations claim to be unique, and often are unique to some extent, but military organizations exhibit characteristics that just are not found in Corporate America. Military leaders send their subordinates into battle. A commander may say to a soldier, "I want you to take that hill, the enemy will be shooting at you, and you will likely die." And the soldier will take the hill. Military commanders must be able to fully control subordinate behavior and, with rare exceptions, they do. They demand almost complete obedience from their subordinates.

To make such obedience possible, the military is carefully engineered to make insubordination unlikely even when orders are questionable. The first step/component to ensuring that orders are followed occurs in basic training. Van Maanen and Schein describe different types of training and the type of behavior each type yields.[2] Investiture training is particularly powerful, and basic training is often used to describe it. A recruit's individual identity is torn down and the recruit is "rebuilt" as best suits the military organization. An interesting description of this can be found in a newspaper article entitled, "Welcome to the Air Force Academy. You're doing everything wrong!"[3] The training has been shown to increase both organizational commitment and cohesion. Additionally, military recruits learn to do what they are told and to not question authority. In fact, when questioned by an underclassman, basic and freshman cadets at the USAFA must respond with one of the following basic responses: (a) Yes, sir! (or Ma'am, as appropriate), (b) No, sir!, (c) No excuse, sir!, (d) Sir, may I ask a question? (e) Sir, may I make a statement? (f) Sir, I do not understand! or (g) Sir, I do not know! From our experience we know that the 4th response, "Sir, may I ask a question?" often yields a "No!" as an answer. One learns very quickly that disobeying or questioning authority is not an option.

During training, and reinforced after, recruits learn of Article 92: Failure to Obey Order or Regulation of the Uniform Code of Military

Justice (UCMJ). According to the code, the maximum punishment for failing to obey an order or regulation is, "(1) *Violation or failure to obey lawful general order or regulation.* Dishonorable discharge, forfeiture of all pay and allowances, and confinement for 2 years. (2) *Violation of failure to obey other lawful order.* Bad-conduct discharge, forfeiture of all pay and allowances, and confinement for 6 months." Of course, there is good reason to create an organizational system whereby rules are followed to a fault. Much of what the military does during the time of war is not pleasant, yet needs to be done. Having a military force follow their orders without question is essential and necessary.

The willingness to do what one is told extends to mere suggestions by the superiors. In classroom discussions with recent USAFA graduates, we often hear stories about colonels suggesting that young lieutenants take on a task; sometimes those lieutenants, thinking that it was only a suggestion and not an order, find themselves under fire for not doing what they were told. It turns out that "suggestions" by high ranking officers are tantamount to orders.

Owing to the extreme pressure to do what one is told, incidents have occurred where unlawful orders were followed causing great harm. One example is the My Lai Massacre where Lt. Calley gave an unlawful order to his soldiers to shoot noncombatant Vietnamese villagers and, unfortunately, they did. Consequently, military members are now trained on what constitutes a lawful order and of their obligation to not follow unlawful orders. GVV falls right in line with this and could easily be incorporated into required training on lawful orders.

Also aligned with the mission and purpose of GVV is the US Military's focus on its core values, particularly integrity. All of the US Military branches include integrity as one of their primary core values. Like the need to obey, it is critical that military members conduct themselves with integrity. Lives truly are at stake and everyone is aware of this.

So, GVV may be useful for military leaders and teachers to use to bridge the gap for military members between obeying the rules and commands of their leaders and the need to speak up when they sense breaches of integrity.

Ethics Curriculum

One primary purpose of ethics training at USAFA is to help cadets internalize the US Air Force's core values: Integrity First, Service before Self, Excellence in all We Do. At the USAFA, we have a Cadet Development Directorate charged with providing character development training to each academic class. Each class receives 8 hours of training each of their 4 years at USAFA. The workshop for freshman, Vital Effective Character Through Observation and Reflection (VECTOR), focuses on personal growth and values through reflection. Sophomores attend a workshop called Respect and Responsibility (R&R) where they gain insight into themselves and learn to develop effective interpersonal relationships that help create healthy command environments. Juniors attend Leaders in Flight Today (LIFT) where one of the key topics is moral courage. Academy Character Enrichment Seminar (ACES) is for seniors and focuses on leading ethically as an Air Force officer.[4]

In addition to the series of ethics training workshops and seminars, USAFA emphasizes the importance of ethics throughout its academic curriculum. Courses in the curriculum are tied to USAFA's Educational Outcomes, two of which focus on ethics—commitment to the "professional and individual responsibility of ethical reasoning and action," and the knowledge of "ethics and the foundation of character."[5] Courses are sequenced so that students' experience and academic coursework leads to the course of instruction in subsequent courses. Our course, Management and Command, is taken by students in their senior year and preceded by courses in behavioral sciences and leadership and philosophy. Specifically, Management and Command:

> . . . introduces students to the complex and dynamic nature of the world in which Air Force officers operate. Through content that is linked to systems theory, this interactive course focuses on the successful techniques that allow officers to understand and influence their environment. Using various models and processes, cadets will explore the interrelationships of power and the context within which it occurs. Students will gain insights into how to make decisions for situations that involve complexity and uncertainty.

The tools are applied to both military and nonmilitary scenarios, with an emphasis on the transition from the cadet role to the role of an officer. In addition, this course is a primary contributor to the development and assessment of the following USAFA outcomes: Responsibilities—Lifelong Development and Contributions, Skills—Decision Making, and Knowledge—Ethics and the Foundations of Character.[6]

There are two prerequisite courses. First is Foundations for Leadership and Character Development, taught by the Department of Behavioral Sciences, which:

> . . . explores leadership development through both academic study and applied exercises. Specifically, the course examines individual leader development principles that will set students on a lifelong path of becoming a leader of character who treats others with respect and dignity. The academic study of leadership development will be combined with experiential exercises, case studies, and student projects designed to help students develop in their own leadership capacity. In addition, this course is a primary contributor to the development and assessment of the following USAFA outcomes: Responsibilities—Respect for Human Dignity and Lifelong Development and Contributions.[7]

The second prerequisite course is Ethics, which is taught by the Department of Philosophy. The course description reads:

> A critical study of several major moral theories and their application to contemporary moral problems with special emphasis on the moral problems of the profession of arms. Highlighted are the officer's responsibilities to reason and act ethically; develop critical thinking skills; know civic, cultural, and international contexts in which the U.S. military operates; and learn influential normative theories about ethics and the foundations of character. In addition, this course is a primary contributor to the development and assessment of the following USAFA outcomes: Responsibilities—Ethical

Reasoning and Action, Skills—Critical Thinking, and Knowledge—Civic, Cultural, and International Environments, and Ethics and the Foundation of Character.[8]

Thus, students enter our course with a strong academic foundation and understanding of the moral theories underlying ethical behavior and motivation to become a military professional dedicated to integrity and respect for human dignity. We also emphasize the Department of Management's commitment to providing a safe environment for our students to express their beliefs through our Human Relations Climate Policy:

As a member of this class, you are expected to "show and receive respect for all people regardless of their race, religion, gender, national origin, color, or status." Such respect specifically precludes any type of harassment, inappropriate comments, or hostile environment. We expect the climate in all Department of Management classrooms to be professional at all times and we expect you to do your part in making this happen.

The policy goes on to advise students to contact their instructor, other professors of the department who are designated Climate Advocates, or the Department Head if they feel uncomfortable or have concerns about classroom discussions and appears on all Department of Management syllabi. However, even with this commitment to foster an environment conducive to students' expressions related to ethics, and as can happen in any course discussing personal decisions and behavior related to ethics, broaching students' beliefs and behavior can be awkward.

GVV provides our faculty in the Management and Command course a mechanism for discussing students' choices in addressing ethical issues. At the same time, it provides our students an opportunity and context to discuss potentially sensitive issues. From studies of bystanders and the social proof literature, we can see that it is difficult to take "correct" action when in the presence of a crowd. GVV, when presented in a class setting, gives students the experience of voicing values while in the presence of peers who may not share their viewpoint. In several instances, it took one brave student to raise their hand and announce they would confront and challenge an ethically dubious position. Once this happened, several other students would join the initial student in agreement to that course of action.

GVV in the Classroom—Early Findings

Although we used aspects of GVV throughout our course, we designated one lesson to have an explicit focus on it. This lesson occurred after we introduced some major themes of the course, including sense making, systems thinking and design, and organizational culture. We specifically introduced GVV in order to reframe these discussions with an ethical perspective.

During this lesson we incorporated the paper Dr. Gentile (see Appendix for excerpt on autonomy versus authority) wrote in conjunction with her visit to the Air Force Academy for the February, 2012, National Character & Leadership Symposium Scholars forum. The reading focused on the tension between authority and autonomy, and Gentile believes this tension might be particularly evident in military contexts. This formed the basis for the in-class discussion, which generated a few themes, and, although anecdotal, are informative.

Theme 1: The cadets here are regularly exposed to a variety of ethics education from several different sources, as previously described. Most in our class identified with "ethics fatigue," a feeling Dr. Gentile referred to in her paper, which emerges from an ethics education pedagogy that is generally abstract and deals with mostly ethical reasoning, theory, and grand dilemmas that are not often encountered in the day-to-day existence of cadets.[9] Reflecting this idea, the general feeling among our students initially seemed to be along the lines of "oh no, not another ethics lesson." In fact, when instructors announced that our next lesson will be on ethics, many students rolled their eyes and others looked defeated as if any chance of an interesting lesson was now lost. Instructors simply smiled and said, "This is going to be different, I think you'll like it."

They did like it. The approach was different from typical lessons on ethics in that the "Tale of Two Stories" forced students to reflect on their experiences rather than contrived textbook examples and cases. Stressing that the lesson is more about their reality than about meeting a lesson objective, instructors were able to gain lesson acceptance rather quickly.

Theme 2: Students see a "disconnect" between theoretical bright lines in academic situations and contextually based gray areas in their actual experiences. They feel that much of what is presented to them does not prepare them for the challenging situations they expect to encounter in "real life." One of the reasons the "Tale of Two Stories" exercise was effective in the classroom was most likely due to the fact that the lines discussed were the lines drawn by our students. Students chose their own examples of success and failure and worked with them as a starting point. Many students made comments like, "I'm not sure this really involves ethics, but ..." They felt free to work with issues that were important to them.

Theme 3: The authority–autonomy tension is real, and there is a strong desire to have autonomy and act as a self-governing agent in these challenging situations. Many students commented that despite the Air Force Academy being a self-labeled "Leadership Laboratory," most often the structure of the system and the detailed instructions concerning activities limited, if not eliminated, chances to express autonomous leadership. Of course, the tension between authority and autonomy exists in all organizations at some level. Bringing this tension out into the open explicitly was critical to the success of the lesson. That was the main reason why the students had read about this tension as a homework assignment before class.

At the start of class, we asked, "What did you think about the reading that discusses the tension between authority and autonomy?" Students responded that there is very little autonomy and we used that as the starting point for our discussions. It turns out that there is always an option to exercise one's autonomy, but it could come at a significant cost if it is not aligned with desires of those in authority. Again, this was an important discussion to have in the classroom as it deals with the reality of their experience rather than theoretical distinctions.

As a practical application to reinforce the discussion and emergent themes, we had the students separate into groups of four and complete the "A Tale of Two Stories" exercise.[10] This particular lesson asks students to contrast a time when their values conflicted with a situation and they did not speak up with a time when they had conflict and they did speak up. This retrospective exercise could be somewhat risky for a cadet because of the honor code they live under, which has a no toleration clause.[11] The course instructors framed these situations as those times when rules were being violated, but no honor code violations were present. We wanted to avoid a potential situation where a cadet might inadvertently implicate himself or herself of tolerating an honor violation.

Beyond the general themes presented earlier, instructors noted common responses during the exercise. In particular, students indicated they were motivated to speak up when they had low toleration for the act they witnessed or empathy for the person who was the victim of the act or when they witnessed unlawful behavior. Students were less likely to speak up when the person committing the act was a friend, had higher military rank than they did, or they felt their speaking up would have no impact on the situation or the probability of its future occurrence.

Students expressed great satisfaction when they spoke up in contrast to dissatisfaction when they chose to not speak up. The circumstances or conditions that would have made speaking up easier for students included having more personal courage/confidence to speak up and not caring what others think about speaking up in alignment with their personal values. A primary objective of the GVV approach would be to also make speaking up easier by means of prescripting, action planning, and actual rehearsal or practice for doing so, coupled with peer coaching to make their approaches more likely to succeed.

We followed up the GVV lesson with a lesson reviewing the Milgram Studies and the Stanford Prison Experiments. Many students had previously seen these well-known studies, but we encouraged them to use the new GVV lens to interpret their meaning. We asked the students if they had different views of how our need to fulfill roles or obey authority affects the desire and ability to speak up in unethical situations.

In addition to in-class discussions, we also ask students to prepare personal journals on several lessons to reflect on course topics that might allow them to see their daily experience from a different perspective. Many students chose to reflect on the meaning of the GVV lesson in this way.

Conclusion

The USAFA's mission is "to educate, train, and inspire men and women to become leaders of character, motivated to lead the United States Air Force in service to our nation," and faculty and staff take this mission very seriously. The stakes are too high to do otherwise. Even though ethics training has been embedded into every aspect of a cadet's education and training, we found that the GVV program is a great addition to that curriculum and does an excellent job of helping cadets deal with the tension between authority and autonomy that sometimes exists in organizations that require a high level of obedience along with a need to voice their values when necessary. Our preliminary experience suggests that we should devote more class time to the GVV curriculum and will likely incorporate scripting into future lessons.

Appendix[12]

What About the Authority/Autonomy Tension?

The challenge with applying the GVV methodology—and its emphasis on rehearsal for voicing and enacting our values—in a military or corporate contexts, as opposed to academic settings, goes precisely to the authority/autonomy tension. That is, is it really values-driven leadership—or even leadership, full stop—if we are just following the rules? Doesn't leadership begin when we need to step out and make choices and inspire confidence and action that is not clear or easy? And if we are engaging students in the process of practicing voicing and enacting values-based choices that are presented as "givens" in the GVV case scenarios, does this become more an exercise in mere compliance than in actual values-driven choice?

This tension between respect for authority, on the one hand, and the need for individual thinking and autonomous choice, on the other, is present in all organizational settings, of course. It becomes especially critical in a military context, where arguably the consequences for both bucking chain-of-command, and also for failing to question that same command and assuming autonomous leadership when required, can be much higher. This assertion was brought home to me when I read about a course in "when and how to disobey orders" at West Point. I presume that there are similar discussions/offerings at USAFA.

Although the GVV curriculum and pedagogical approach has enjoyed much more rapid and enthusiastic adoption that we had dared expect, one of the most important challenges it has faced is precisely around this tension. If GVV is about learning and practicing to voice and enact values effectively, what if the values one learns to enact are "bad values" ? This can of course refer to "bad rules" or "immoral directives" coming from the seat of organizational authority: That is, occasions when resisting pressures to break the rules may be the less ethical choice. On the other hand, this challenge to GVV can also refer to the danger of equipping individuals to buck authority when they should not do so—going rogue, if you will.

In the end, there is no easy answer to this tension; it is a matter of judgment and of situational factors. However, I want to suggest that it is precisely in a context like the USAFA—where the stakes are so high, both for a failure to obey authority as well as for a failure to question illegitimate or unethical authority—that using the GVV process to provide students with opportunities to learn and practice constructive, effective, persuasive, non-polarizing ways to raise values-based positions may be most powerful and the most inspiring model for other settings, such as the corporate world.

In fact, I would suggest that the more obedience to authority is required in a particular context, the more responsibility and even necessity there is in that same setting to provide opportunities for true deliberation and even debate. It is this open discussion that enables individual to truly understand the meaning, the purpose, and the intent behind the rules and behavioral norms and hierarchy, such that they can both more fully respect and embrace it but also understand when it is truly at risk from authority illegitimately enacted.

If I were to see my fondest hope to materialize from this Symposium, it would be to see this methodology of *team-based "scripting," action-planning, practice and peer coaching* applied to the voicing of values, both around resisting pressures to violate the legitimate rules and norms and authority of the military, as well as around resisting the pressures that can come directly from rules and norms inappropriately applied.

Notes

Chapter 1

1. For a more detailed explanation of this curriculum and the thinking and research behind it, see *Giving Voice to Values: How to Speak Your Mind When You Know What's Right* (Yale University Press, 2010, www.GivingVoiceTo ValuesTheBook.com) and "Values-Driven Leadership Development: Where We Have Been and Where We Could Go," *Organization Management Journal* (2012), *9*(3), 188–196, both by Mary C. Gentile. For the free, download-able GVV Curriculum, see www.GivingVoiceToValues.org.
2. See especially "Ways of Thinking About Our Values in the Workplace," available at www.GivingVoiceToValues.org.
3. See the GVV case, "Jeff Salett: From the Top, Sort Of" at www.GivingVoiceTo Values.org.

Chapter 2

1. "As regards *market prices*, Supply is taken to mean the stock of the com-modity in question which is at hand, or at all events 'in sight' (p. 378); *As a general rule*, the shorter the period which we are considering, the greater must be the share of our attention given to the influence of demand on value (p. 349);" Marshall (1961), emphasis in the original.
2. In addition, see DeAlessi (1975); Douty (1972); Hirshleifer (1963, 1987); Kahneman et al. (1986).
3. Arce and Li (2011) provide contextual data showing that those who choose not to select the profit-maximizing level of layoffs understand and reject the profit-maximization criterion when it comes to layoffs during a recession.
4. Waffle House prices are set regionally and vary by season. Former Waffle House president and CEO Bert Thompson describes the limited menu as, "You can have anything you want; here's the list of what you're going to want," (Ergun et al. 2010, p. 117).
5. See Hirshleifer (1963, 1987); Kunreuther and Fiore (1966); Kunreuther (1967); Douty (1972); De Alessi (1975); Neilson (2009).

Chapter 3

1. Laszlo, and Zhexembayeva (2011); Werbach (2009); Epstein (2008).
2. Lueneburger and Goleman (2010).
3. Gentile (2010b).
4. *Inheriting a Complex World: Future Leaders Envision Sharing the Planet.* (2010).
5. Hopkins (2009).
6. Lovins, Lovins, and Hawken (1999).
7. Gentile (2010a), p. 31.
8. Gentile (2010a), pp. 24–46.
9. Porter and Kramer (2011).
10. Gentile (2010a), p. 28.
11. Gentile (2010a), p. 4.
12. Gentile (2010c).
13. Bandura (1993).
14. Wood and Bandura (1989), p. 365.
15. Bandura (1989), p. 365.
16. Bandura (1989), p. 365.
17. Gentile (2010d).
18. Gentile (2010b).
19. Gentile (2010e).
20. See Gentile (2010a), Appendix C.
21. Zadek (2004).
22. Kotter and Cohen (2002).

Chapter 4

1. The SEC has delegated the responsibility to the accounting profession to establish generally accepted accounting principles, or GAAP. The Financial Accounting Standards Board (FASB) is the current standard-setter for the profession. The SEC does establish financial reporting and disclosure standards under *Regulation S-X* that ultimately must be adhered to by all public companies in their annual 10-K reports filed with the Commission. The SEC regulates the audit of public companies through the Public Company Accounting Oversight Board (PCAOB), an independent body established after the fallout from accounting scandals at companies such as Enron and WorldCom.
2. Gentile (2010).
3. ACFE (2012), p. 4.
4. ACFE (2012), pp. 29–31.
5. Rest (1986).

Chapter 5

1. Härtel and Fujimoto (2010); Pennington, Macklin, and Campbell (2007); Simmons (2008).
2. Searl et al. (2011); Lewicki, Tomlinson, and Gillispie (2006); Wang and Noe (2010).
3. Cerne, Nerstad, Dysvik, and Škerlavaj (2013).
4. Härtel (2008).
5. Arnsten, Mazure, and Sinha (2012).
6. Gentile (2010).
7. Gentile (2010).
8. Gentile (2010), p. 114.
9. Gentile (2010), p. 62.
10. Gentile (2010), p.147.
11. Gentile (2010), pp. 147–153.
12. Gentile (2010), pp. 3–23.
13. Budiman, Roan, and Callan (2012).
14. Gentile (2010), p. 219.

Chapter 6

1. Parker (1965).
2. Roberts, Brown, and Olsen (2011).
3. Many governments in developed countries are now publishing regular state of the service reports which are similar to climate surveys conducted in the private sector. See, for example, Roan (2011).

Chapter 7

1. See Honeyman et al. (2009), p. 2.
2. As an example, the American Bar Association's Section of Dispute Resolution regularly offers a Legal Educators' Colloquium—a series of sessions devoted to negotiation and dispute resolution education—at its annual conference (see http://www.americanbar.org/groups/dispute_resolution/events_cle/15th_annual_sectionofdisputeresolutionspringconference/session_descriptions/legal_educators_colloquium.html). The Dispute Resolution Research Center at Northwestern University's Kellogg School of Management offers a semiannual teaching conference on negotiation and teamwork, along with a series of webinars on teaching negotiation (see http://www.kellogg.northwestern.edu/research/drrc/events/past-conferences.aspx). The Program on Negotiation at Harvard Law School publishes a periodic

newsletter on teaching negotiation (see http://archive.constantcontact.com/ fs079/1101638633053/archive/1102166412934.html). Between 2009 and 2012, Hamline University School of Law, JAMS Foundation, The Leading Negotiation institute, Convenor Conflict Management, and ADR Center Italy hosted conferences in Rome, Istanbul, and Beijing focused on defining and developing the next generation of negotiation education (see http://law. hamline.edu/rethinkingNegotiation.html).

3. Cf. Wheeler (2006)—observing that teaching negotiation is easy in terms of engaging participants and garnering positive ratings, but hard in terms of grappling with truly complex issues such as ethics and bias and ensuring that students actually retain and apply what they learn.

4. See Schneider and Honeyman (2006).

5. See Honeyman et al. (2013), chapters 17–21 on "Teaching Wicked Problems"; Wheeler (2006).

6. See Ebner et al. (2012).

7. See, e.g., Nadler et al. (2003), comparing four common negotiation teaching methods and finding that analogical learning most improved students ability to conceptually analyze a negotiation but observational learning most improved substantive performance (possibly via tacit knowledge).

8. See Wheeler (2000), section II on Curriculum Design provides an overview of typical negotiation course content in schools and programs of business, law, public administration, environmental studies, and conflict resolution.

9. Englund and Jordan (1990), Track 8 ("Final Chances").

10. NASA is the National Aeronautic and Space Administration, a civilian space exploration program created by the United States government in 1958. Morton Thiokol is the engineering firm that NASA contracted to design and build reusable solid rocket boosters for the shuttle orbiters.

11. See Lax and Sebenius (2006).

12. The readings included chapter 7 ("Strategies of Influence") in Malhotra and Bazerman (2008a), which addresses influence techniques such as highlighting potential losses rather than gains, the "door in the face" and "foot in the door" approaches, and the power of justification, as well as several strategies for resisting influence; and an excerpt from Lax and Sebenius (2006), outlining a "3-D" approach to negotiation that incorporates direct interpersonal tactics, substantive deal design, and away-from-the-table "setup" moves such as coalition-building and development of alternatives to a negotiated agreement. The GVV *Scripts and Skills* module includes several other suggested readings regarding decision biases and heuristics, influence strategies, changing minds, and related topics.

13. These readings included chapters 4 ("When Rationality Fails: Biases of the Mind") and 5 ("When Rationality Fails: Biases of the Heart") in Malhotra

and Bazerman (2008a), addressing common decision-making biases such as escalation of commitment, vividness, egocentrism, overconfidence, self-serving attributions, and regret aversion.

14. Englund and Jordan (1990), track 8 ("Final Chances"). While the film is a made-for-television dramatization rather than a documentary, I use this excerpt because it tends to engage students more thoroughly than a standard written case study, and vividly depicts some of the communication difficulties inherent in a 32-person telephonic negotiation in three different locations. The dialogue in this excerpt relatively accurately reflects subsequent testimony about the actual dialogue, as recounted in the Rogers Commission Report (1986). Many alternate materials describing the *Challenger* launch negotiations are available (e.g., Rogers Commission Report (1986); Edmondson and Feldman (2002); Youngdahl (2011)).

15. See Lax and Sebenius (2006); see also Watkins (2007).

16. See Malhotra and Bazerman (2008a), chpts. 4, 5, and 7 for a discussion of psychological biases and influence strategies.

17. See Lax and Sebenius (2006); Watkins (2007).

18. See Babcock and Laschever (2007), ch. 1 ("Opportunity doesn't always knock").

19. Within the 3-D negotiation framework, this is an example of integrating third-dimension (setup) with first-dimension (table tactics) moves. See Lax and Sebenius (2006).

20. See Brown and Duguid (1989).

21. See Williams et al. (2008).

22. See Malhotra and Bazerman (2008b), noting that the integration of influence studies into the negotiation field is "long overdue".

23. See, e.g., Menkel-Meadow and Wheeler (2004); Wheeler (2004); Lewicki et al. (2010), ch. 9, "Ethics in Negotiation"; Wash (2006); Gibson (2006).

24. See Bernard (2010), p. 64.

25. See, e.g., Menkel-Meadow and Wheeler (2004); Wheeler (2004); Lewicki et al. (2010); Walsh (2006); Gibson (2006).

26. See, e.g., Stone et al. (2010), chapter 2 ("Stop Arguing about Who's Right"); Lax and Sebenius (2006), chapter 5 ("Get All the Interests Rights").

27. See Wheeler (2004); Menkel-Meadow and Wheeler (2004).

Chapter 8

1. Hafrey (2005).

2. Gentile (2010), p. 7.

3. Rusesabagina (2006), pp. xiv–xv.

4. Rusesabagina (2006), p. 202.

Chapter 9

1. Ashcraft (2001); Mirabella and Wish (2001); Warren and Rosenthal (2006).
2. Warren and Rosenthal (2006).
3. Ashcraft (2001); Mirabella and Wish (2001); Warren and Rosenthal (2006).
4. Bornstein (2007).
5. Warren and Rosenthal (2006).
6. Kickul and Lyons (2012).
7. Eikenberry and Kluver (2004).
8. Peredo and McClean (2006).
9. Dees (1998); Peredo and McClean (2006); Weerawardena and Sullivan Mort (2006); Santos (2009).
10. The opinion reflected in a number of contributions is that the relatively recent growth in the social economy sector is a result of socioeconomic crisis within the public and private sectors (Moulaert and Ailenei (2005)) fuelled by the demise of the welfare state and the emergence of welfare markets, creating a range of "enterprises with social purpose" (Laville (2003); Powell and Barrientos (2004); Spear and Bidet (2005)).
11. Chaves and Monzon (2007).
12. Eikenberry and Kluver (2004).
13. Young (2001); Ashforth and Mael (1996); Corley (2004); Harrow and Mole (2005); Clegg et al. (2007).
14. Dutton et al. (1994).
15. Zack (2003); Wilhelm (2006); Holtfreter (2008); Strickland and Vaughan (2008).
16. Menzel (1997), as cited in Jurkiewicz and Massey (1998).
17. Etzioni (1987); Bhide and Stevenson (1990).
18. Holtfreter (2008).
19. Zahra et al. (2009).
20. Etzioni (1987); Bhide and Stevenson (1990).
21. Zahra et al. (2009).
22. Crossan et al. (2012).
23. Gentile (2010).
24. Gentile (2010), Chapter 3.
25. Crossan et al. (2012).
26. Gentile (2010).

Chapter 10

1. Srinivasan (2006).
2. Basu (2008).
3. Central Vigilance Commission (2010).

4. See "The business of integrity: a panel discussion on how corporate India can help solve the problem of corruption" (April 2012).
5. Maak and Pless (2006).
6. Doh and Tyman (2011).
7. Gaur (2006).
8. Maak et al. (2006).
9. Whetten and Delbecq (2000).
10. Freeman and Auster (2011).
11. Krishnan, Reddy, Srinivasan, and Jaiswal (2011).
12. Krishnan et al. (2011).
13. Olila (2000).
14. The course was called "Life as a Leader" to differentiate it from existing electives on Leadership.
15. March and Weil (2005).
16. Donghoon, Yigang, and Heung (1998).
17. Supplementary articles on Leadership were used when necessary.
18. This was necessary for students who were weak in English.
19. Articles were sourced from Rhode (2006).
20. A 1999 film directed by Michael Mann for Spyglass Entertainment.
21. They felt that the builder may have acquired the land from a private party and therefore might have paid the market rate for the property. It was only fair that he recovered what he invested.
22. Many participants suggested that the politician should be isolated from the process!!

Chapter 11

1. Gentile (2010).
2. This section is based on Gentile (2010) case.
3. Plambeck and Denand (2010).
4. Additional guidelines for teaching are provided in the Gentile (2010) Teaching Note.

Chapter 12

1. The Hindu (2012).
2. IIM Bangalore (2012).
3. Sarin (2012).
4. LRN (2010).
5. Kotler, Keller, Koshi, and Jha (2009).

Chapter 13

1. *The views expressed in this article are those of the authors and do not necessarily reflect the official policy or position of the United States Air Force Academy, Air Force, Department of Defense, or the US Government.*
2. Van Maanen and Schein (1979).
3. Terdiman (2009).
4. http://www.usafa.edu/Commandant/cwc/cwcx.cfm?catname=cwc.
5. http://www.usafa.edu/df/data/USAFA%20Outcomes.pdf.
6. USAFA Curriculum Handbook (2012–2013), p. 308.
7. USAFA Curriculum Handbook (2012–2013), p. 238.
8. USAFA Curriculum Handbook (2012–2013), p. 333.
9. Gentile (2012).
10. Gentile (2010).
11. USAFA Honor Code: "We Will Not Lie, Steal Or Cheat, Nor Tolerate Among Us Anyone Who Does" (http://www.usafa.af.mil/information/factsheets/factsheet.asp?id=9427)
12. Gentile (2012).

References

American Institute of Cpas (AICPA). (2012). *Professional standards volume 2.* New York: AICPA.

Aragon, G. A. (2011). *Financial ethics. A positivist analysis.* Oxford: Oxford University Press.

Arce, D. G. (2004). Conspicuous by its absence: Ethics and managerial economics. *Journal of Business Ethics 54*(3), 259–275.

Arce, D. G. (2005). Subgame perfection and the ethics of competition. *Managerial and Decision Economics 26*(6), 397–405.

Arce, D.G. (2011). Giving voice to values in economics and finance. *Journal of Business Ethics Education 8,* 343–347.

Arce, D. G., & Li, S. X. (2011). Profits, layoffs, and priorities. *Journal of Business Ethics 101*(1), 49–60.

Arnsten, A., Mazure, C. M., & Sinha, R. (2012, April). This is your brain. *Scientific American 306,* 48–53.

Ashcraft, R. F. (2001). Where nonprofit management meets the undergraduate experience: American humanics after 50 years, *Public Performance and Management Review 25*(1), 42–56.

Ashforth, B. E., & Mael, F. (1989). Social identity theory and the organization. *The Academy of Management Review 14*(1), 20–39.

Association of Certified Fraud Examiners (ACFE) (2012). *Report to the Nations on Occupational Fraud and Abuse: 2012 Global Fraud Survey.* Retrieved from Acfe Website: http://www.acfe.com/uploadedFiles/ACFE_Website/Content/rttn/2012-report-to-nations.pdf

Babcock, L., & Laschever S. (2007). *Women don't ask: The high cost of avoiding negotiation—and positive strategies for change* (paperback ed.). New York: Bantam Dell.

Bandura A. (1993). Perceived self-efficacy in cognitive development and functioning. *Educational Psychologist 28,* 117–148.

Basu, K. (2008). India's dilemmas: The political economy of policy making in a globalized world. *Economic and Political Weekly XLIII*(5), 33–62.

Bauerlein, V. (2011, September 1). How to measure a storm's fury one breakfast at a time. *The Wall Street Journal 1.*

Bazerman, M. H., & Tenbrunsel, A. E. (2011). *Blind spots. Why we fail to do what's right and what to do about it.* Princeton, NJ: Princeton University Press.

Bernard, P. E. (2010). Reorienting the trainer to navigate—not negotiate—Islamic cultural values. Chapter 4. In C. Honeyman & J. Coben (Eds.), *Venturing beyond the classroom: Volume 2 in the rethinking negotiation teaching series* (pp. 61–76). St. Paul, MN: DRI Press.

Bhide, A., & Stevenson, H. H. (1990). Why be honest if honesty doesn't pay?, *Harvard Business Review 68*(5), 2–9.

Bornstein (2007). *How to change the world: Social entrepreneurs and the power of new ideas,* Oxford: Oxford University Press, Inc

Brown, J. S., Collins, A., & Duguid, P. (1989). Situated cognition and the culture of learning. *Educational Researcher 18*(1), 32–42.

Budiman, A., Roan, A., & V. J. Callan (2012, August). Rationalizing ideologies, social identities and corruption among civil servants in Indonesia during the Suharto era. *Journal of Business Ethics.* Retrieved from Springer Website http://link.springer.com.ezproxy.library.uq.edu.au/article/10.1007/s10551-012-1451-y/fulltext.html

Central Vigilance Commission (2010). *Annual Report: 1.1.2010 to 31.12.2010.* Retrieved on February 11, 2013, from Cvc Website: http://www.cvc.nic.in/ar2010_01092011.pdf

Cerne, M., Nerstad, C., Dysvik, A., & Škerlavaj, M. (2013). What goes around comes around: Knowledge hiding, perceived motivational climate, and creativity. *Academy of Management Journal,* published ahead of print January 4, 2013, DOI: 10.5465/amj.2012.0122.

Clegg, S. R., Rhodes, C., & Kornberger, M. (2007). Desperately seeking legitimacy: Organizational identity and emerging industries. *Organization Studies 28*(4), 495–513.

Corley, K. G. (2004). Defined by our strategy or our culture? Hierarchical differences in perceptions of organizational identity and change. *Human Relations 57*(9), 1145–1177.

Crossan, D., Ibbotson, P., & Bell, J. D. (2012). "Social entrepreneurs: The Hologram effect", *Journal of Small Business and Enterprise Development* pending publication *19*(1).

De Alessi, L. (1975). Toward an analysis of postdisaster cooperation. *American Economic Review 65*(1), 127–138.

Dees, J. G. (1998). *The meaning of 'social entrepreneurship*, Working Paper, Stanford University, Graduate School of Business, California.

Doh, S., & Tyman, Jr. (2011). Responsible leadership helps retain talent in India. *Journal of Business Ethics 98*, 85–100.

Donghoon, K., Yigang, P., & Heung, S. P. (1998). High- versus low-context culture: A comparison of Chinese, Korean & American cultures. *Psychology and Marketing 15*(6), 507–521.

Douty, C. M. (1972). Disasters and charity: Some aspects of cooperative economic behavior. *American Economic Review 62*(4), 580–590.

Dutton, J. E., Dukerich, J. M. & Harquail, C. V. (1994). Organizational images and member identification. *Administrative Sciences Quarterly 39*, 239–263.

Ebner, N., Coben J., & Honeyman C. (Eds.). (2012). *Assessing our students, assessing ourselves: Volume 3 in the rethinking negotiation teaching series.* St. Paul, MN: DRI Press.

Edmonson, A. E., & Feldman, L. R. (2002). Group process in the *Challenger* launch decision (A–D). Boston, MA: Harvard Business School Publishing (Product # 603068/70/72/73-PDF-ENG).

Eikenberry, A. M., & Kluver, J. D. (2004). The marketization of the nonprofit sector: Civil society at risk? *Public Administration Review 64*(2), 132–140.

Englund, G., & Jordan, G. (1990). *Challenger.* United States: American Broadcasting Company (original airing).

Epstein, M. J. (2008). *Making sustainability work: Best practices in managing and measuring corporate social, environmental, and economic impacts.* San Francisco, CA: Greenleaf Publishing.

Ergun, O., Heierstamm, J. L., Keskinocak, P., & Swann, J. L. (2010). Waffle House restaurants hurricane response: A case study. *International Journal of Production Economics 126*(1), 111–120.

Eriksson, R. (2005). On the ethics of environmental economics as seen from textbooks. *Ecological Economics 52*(4), 421–435.

Etzioni, A. (1987). Entrepreneurship, adaptation and legitimization. *Journal of Economic Behaviour and Organization 8*, 175–189.

Ferraro, F., Pfeffer, J., & Sutton, R. I. (2005). Economic language and assumptions: How theories can become self-fulfilling. *Academy of Management Review 30*(1), 8–24.

Frank, R. (2004). *What price the moral high ground? Ethical dilemmas in competitive environments.* Princeton, NJ: Princeton University Press.

Freeman, R. E., & Auster, E. R. (2011). Values, authenticity and responsible leadership. *Journal of Business Ethics 98*, 15–23.

Friedman, M. (1970, September 13). The social responsibility of the firm is to increase its profits. *New York Times, Sunday Magazine,* pp. 32, 33, 122, 126.

Gaur, A. (2006). Changing demands of leaders in the new economy: A survey of Indian leaders. *IIMB Management Review 18*(2), 149–158.

Gentile, M. C. (2010a). *Giving voice to values: How to speak your mind when you know what's right.* New Haven and London: Yale University Press.

Gentile, M. C. (2010b). "*Teaching note for this whole system seems wrong": Felipe Montez and concerns about the global supply chain. Retrieved from* Giving Voice to Values Website: http://www.babson.edu/faculty/teaching-learning/gvv/Pages/home

Gentile, M. (2010c). "*This Whole System Seems Wrong": Felipe Montez and concerns about the global supply chain. Retrieved* December 14, 2012, from

Giving Voice to Values Curriculum Materials Website: http://www.babson. edu/faculty/teaching-learning/gvv/Pages/curriculum.aspx

Gentile, M. C. (2012). Giving voice to values: Tensions between autonomy and authority. *Paper presented at the United States Air Force Academy National Character & Leadership Symposium Scholars' Forum, February 2012*, 1–10.

Gentile, M. C. (2010d). *Reasons and rationalizations*. Retrieved from Giving Voice to Values Website: http://www.GivingVoiceToValues.org.

Gentile, M. C. (2010e). *A tale of two stories*. Retrieved from Giving Voice to Values Website: http://www.GivingVoiceToValues.org.

Gentile, M. C. (2010f). *Guidelines for peer coaching*. Retrieved from Giving Voice to Values Website: http://www.GivingVoiceToValues.org.

Gentile, M. C. (2010g). *The whole system seems wrong*. Retrieved from Giving Voice to Values Website: http://www.GivingVoiceToValues.org.

Gentile, M. C. (2010h). Ways of thinking about our values in the workplace. In M. C. Gentile (Ed.), *Giving voice to values*. Wellesley, MA: Babson College.

Gibson, K. (2006). Ethics and morality in negotiation. In A. K. Schneider & C. Honeyman (Eds.) *The negotiator's field book: The desk reference for the experienced negotiator*, chapter 19. Washington, D.C.: ABA Section of Dispute Resolution.

Gonzalez-Padron, T., Ferrell, O. C., Ferrell L., & Smith, I. A. (2012). A critique of Giving Voice to Values approach to business ethics education. *Journal of Academic Ethics 10*, 251–269.

Hafrey, & Leigh (2005). *The Story of Success: Five Steps to Mastering Ethics in Business*. New York, NY: Other Press.

Harrow, J., & Mole, V. (2005). 'I Want to Move Once I Have Got Things Straight': Voluntary Sector Chief Executives' Career Accounts'. *Nonprofit Management and Leadership 16*(1), 79–100.

Härtel, C. E. J. (2004). Towards a multicultural world: Identifying work systems, practices and employee attitudes that embrace diversity. *The Australian Journal of Management 29*(2), 189–200.

Härtel, C. E. J. (2008). How to build a healthy emotional culture and avoid a toxic culture. In C. L. Cooper & N. M. Ashkanasy (Eds.), *Research Companion to Emotion in Organization* (pp. 575–588). Cheltenham, UK: Edwin Elgar Publishing.

Härtel, C. E. J., & Fujimoto, Y. (2010). *Human resource management* (2nd ed.). Pearson Education Australia. ISBN: 9781442517981.

Hirshleifer, J. (1963). *Disaster and recovery: A historical survey*. RAND Memorandum RM-3079-PR, Santa Monica, CA: RAND.

Hirshleifer, J. (1987). Disaster behavior: Altruism or alliance? In J. Hirshleifer (Ed.), *Economic behavior in adversity* (pp. 134–141). Brighton, CO: University of Chicago Press.

Holtfreter, K. (2008). Determinants of fraud losses in nonprofit organisations. *Nonprofit Management and Leadership, 19*(1), 45–63.

Honeyman, C., Coben J., & De Palo G. (2009). Introduction: The second generation of negotiation teaching. In C. Honeyman, J. Coben, & G. De Palo (Eds.), *Rethinking negotiation teaching: Innovations for content and culture* (chapter 1, pp. 1–12). St. Paul, MN: DRI Press

Honeyman, C., Coben, J., & Lee A. W. (Eds.). (2013). *Educating negotiators for a connected world.* St. Paul, MN: DRI Press.

Hopkins, M. S. (2009). What executives don't get about sustainability (and further notes on the profit motive). *MIT Sloan Management Review 51*(1), 35–40.

Indian Institute of Management Bangalore (2012, March 26). National workshop on teaching of ethics, corporate governance, and corporate social responsibility.

Inheriting a Complex World: Future Leaders Envision Sharing the Planet. (June, 2010). Retrieved August 11, 2012, from IBM Institute for Business Value website: http://public.dhe.ibm.com/common/ssi/ecm/en/gbe03350usen/GBE03350USEN.PDF

Kahneman, D., Knetsch, J. L., & Thaler, R. (1986). Fairness as a constraint on profit seeking: Entitlements in the market. *American Economic Review 76*(4), 728–742.

Kickul, J., & Lyons, T. (2012). *Understanding social entrepreneurship: The relentless pursuit of mission in an ever changing world,* Routledge.

Kotler, P., Keller, K. L., Koshy, A., & Jha, M. (2009). *Marketing management: A South Asian perspective.* (13th ed.). New Delhi: Pearson.

Kotter, J. P., & Cohen, D. S. (2002). *The heart of change: Real-life stories of how people change their organizations.* Boston, MA: Harvard Business Press.

Krishnan, R. T., Reddy, C. M., Srinivasan, V., & Jaiswal, M. K. (2011). The leadership journey at the Murugappa Group. In Shyamsunder, A. et al. *Leadership development in organizations in India: The why and how of it (part II) Vikalpa 36*(4), 77–131.

Kunreuther, H. (1967). The peculiar economics of disaster. *Papers in Non-Market Decision Making 3*(1), 67–83.

Kunreuther, H., & Fiore, E. S. (1966). The Alaskan Earthquake. A case study in the economics of disaster. *Institute for Defense Analyses, Economic and Political Studies Division, Study S-228.* Santa Monica, CA: RAND.

Laszlo, C., & Zhexembayeva, N. (2011). *Embedded sustainability—the next big competitive advantage.* Stanford, CA: Stanford University Press.

Laville J. L. (2003). Childcare and welfare mix in France. *Annals of Public and Cooperative Economics, 74*(4), 591–630

Lax, D., & Sebenius J. (2006). *3-D negotiation: Powerful tools to change the game in your most important deals.* Cambridge, MA: Harvard Business School Press.

Levitt, S. D., & Dubner, S. J. (2005). *Freakonomics*. New York: HarperCollins.

Lewicki, R. J., Barry B., & Saunders D. M. (2010). *Negotiation* (6th ed.). New York: McGraw-Hill.

Lewicki, R., Tomlinson, E., & Gillespie, N. (2006). Models of interpersonal trust development: Theoretical approaches, empirical evidence, and future directions. *Journal of Management 32*(6), 991–1022.

Lovins, L. H., Lovins, A., & Hawken, P. (1999). *Natural capitalism*. Boston, MA: Little, Brown.

LRN Ethics and Compliance leadership Survey Report 2010-11. Retrieved January 28, 2013, from Lrn Website: http://www.lrn.com/sites/default/files/2010_2011_Ethics_and_Compliance_Leadership_Report_0.pdf

Lueneburger, C., & Goleman, D. (2010). The change leadership sustainability demands. *MIT Sloan Management Review 51*(4), 49–55.

Maak, T., & Pless, N. (2006). Responsible leadership in a stakeholder society: A relational perspective. *Journal of Business Ethics 66*, 99–115.

Malhotra, D., & Bazerman M. H. (2008a). *Negotiation genius: How to overcome obstacles and achieve brilliant results at the bargaining table and beyond.* Boston, MA: Harvard Business School Press.

Malhotra, D., & Bazerman M. H. (2008b). Psychological influence in negotiation: An introduction long overdue. *Journal of Management 34*(3), 509–531.

March, J. G., & Weil, T. (2005). *On Leadership*. Oxford, UK: Blackwell Publishing.

Marshall, A. (1961). *Principles of Economics* (9th(Variorum) ed.). New York: MacMillan.

McAdoo, B., & Manwaring M. (2009, April). Teaching for implementation: Designing negotiation curricula to maximize long-term learning. *Negotiation Journal 25*(2), 195–215.

Menkel-Meadow, C., & Wheeler, M. (Eds.). (2004). *What's fair: Ethics for negotiators.* San Francisco, CA: Jossey-Bass.

Menzel (1997), as cited in Jurkiewicz, C. L., & Massey, T. K. (1998). The influence of ethical reasoning on leader effectiveness an empirical study of nonprofit executives. *Nonprofit Management & Leadership*, 9(2), 173–186.

Miller, D. T. (1999). The norm of self-interest. *American Psychologist 54*(12), 1053–1063.

Mirabella, R. M., & Wish, N. B. (2001). University based educational programs in the management of nonprofit organisations: An updated Census of US programs. *Public Performance and Management Review 1*, 30–41.

Moor, R. E. (1987, October 11–14). Ethics for businesses … and their economists. *Business Economics*.

Moulaert, F., & Ailenei, O. (2005). 'Social Economy, Third Sector and Solidarity Relations: a Conceptual Synthesis from History to Present, *Urban Studies 42*(11), 2037–53.

Nadler, J., Thompson L., & van Boven L. (2003). Learning negotiation skills: Four models of knowledge creation and transfer. *Management Science 49*(4), 529–540.

Neilson, H. (2009). Price gouging versus price reduction in retail gasoline markets during Hurricane Rita. *Economics Letters 105*(1), 11–13.

Northrup, E. (2000). Normative foundations of introductory economics. *The American Economist 44*(1), 53–61.

Ollila, S. (2000). Creativity and Innovativeness through reflective project leadership. *Reflective Project Leadership 9*(3), 195–200.

Parker R. S. (1965). Public service neutrality: A moral problem: The Creighton case. In B. B. Schaffer & Corbett D. C. (Eds.), *Decisions: Case Studies in Australian Administration* (p. 205). Sydney: Cheshire.

Patton, B. (2009, October). The deceptive simplicity of teaching negotiation: Reflections on thirty years of the negotiation workshop. *Negotiation Journal 25*(4), 481–498.

Peredo, A. M., & McClean, M. (2006). Social Entrepreneurship: A Critical Review of the Concept. Journal of World Business *41*(2006), 56–65.

Pinnington, A., Macklin, R., & Campbell, T. (Eds.). (2007). *Human resource management: Ethics and employment* (pp. 1–22). Oxford, UK: Oxford University Press.

Plambeck, E., & Denand, L. (2010). *Wal-Mart's sustainability strategy.* HBS No. OIT71-PDF-ENG. Boston, MA: Harvard Business School Publishing.

Porter, M., & Kramer, M. R. (2011). Creating shared value. *Harvard Business Review 89*(1/2), 62–77.

Powell, M., & Barrientos A. (2004). Welfare regimes and the Welfare Mix. *European Journal of Political Research 43*(1), 83–185

Rest, J. R. (1986). *Moral development: Advances in research and theory.* Westport, CT: Praeger Publishers.

Rhode, D. L. (2006). (Ed.) *Moral leadership: The theory and practice of power, judgment, and policy.* San Francisco, CA: Jossey-Bass.

Roan, A. (2011). The state of the service: Comparing the reports from the UK and Australia. *Public Interest: Newsletter of the Institute of Public Administration Australia (Queensland Division) 4*, 17–19.

Roberts, P., Brown A. J., & Olsen, J. (2011). *Whistling while they work: A good-practice guide for managing internal reporting of wrongdoing in public sector organisations.* Retrieved July 12, 2012, from ANU E-Press Website: http://epress.anu.edu.au?p=144611

Rogers Commission Report. 1986. *Report of the Presidential Commission on the Space Shuttle Challenger accident.*

Rubinstein, A. (2006). A sceptic's comment on the study of economics. *The Economic Journal 116*(510), C1–C9.

Rusesabagina, P., & Zoellner, T. (2006). *An ordinary man: An autobiography.* New York, NY: Viking.

Sandel, M. J. (2005). Markets, morals, and civil life. *Bulletin of the American Academy of Arts & Sciences* 6–11.

Santos, F. (2009). *A theory of social entrepreneurship*, Working Paper Series. Retrieved from INSEAD Website: www.insead.edu/se

Sarin, S. (2012). My years with B2B marketing in India: Reflections and learning from a journey of 40 years. *Journal of Business & Industrial Marketing 27*(3), 160–168.

Schneider, A. K., & Honeyman C. (Eds.). (2006). *The negotiator's field book: The desk reference for the experienced negotiator.* Washington, D.C.: The American Bar Association Section of Dispute Resolution.

Searle, R., Den Hartog, D. N., Weibel, A., Gillespie, N., Six, F., Hatzakis, T., & Skinner, D. (2011). Trust in the employer: The role of high-involvement work practices and procedural justice in European organizations. *International Journal of Human Resource Management 22*(5), 1069–1092.

Simmons, J. (2008). Ethics and morality in Human Resource Management. *Social Responsibility Journal 4*(1/2), 8–23.

Spear, R., & Bidet, E. (2005). Social enterprise for work integration in 12 European Countries: A descriptive analysis. *Annals of Public and Cooperative Economics 76*(2).

Srinivasan, T. N. (2006). China, India and the world economy. *Economic and Political Weekly XLI*(34), 3716–3727.

Stone, D., Patton B., & Heen, S. (2010). *Difficult conversations: How to discuss what matters most* (rev. ed.). New York: Penguin Books.

Strickland, R. A., & Vaughan, S. K. (2008). The hierarchy of ethical values in nonprofit organisations: A framework for an ethical, self-actualized organisational culture. *Public Integrity 10*(3), 233–251.

Terdiman, D. (2009, June 26). *Welcome to the Air Force Academy. You're doing everything wrong!* Retrieved December 1, 2012, from CNET.com Website: http://news.cnet.com/8301-13772_3-10273555-52.html

The Business of integrity: A panel discussion on how corporate India can help solve the problem of corruption. (April 2012). Retrieved *January 15, 2013, from* Spencerstuart Website: www.spencerstuart.com/research/1587

The Hindu (2012). *Why the world still chases top B-school grads.* Retrieved January 14, 2013, from The Hindu Businessline Website: http://www.thehindubusinessline.com/news/education/article3738295.ece?homepage=true

United States v. Arthur Young, 465 U.S. 805 (1984). Retrieved from Supreme. justia Website: http://supreme.justia.com/cases/federal/us/465/805/case.html

Van Maanen, J., & Schein, E. H. (1979). Toward a theory of organizational socialization. *Research in Organizational Behavior 1*, 209–264.

Wang, S., & Noe, R. A. (2010). Knowledge sharing: A review and directions for future research. *Human Resource Management Review 20*(2), 115–131.

Warren, B. W., & Rosenthal, D. (2006). Teaching Business Ethics—Is it a Lost Cause?. *International Journal of Management 23*(3 Part 2), 679–698.

Watkins, M. D. (2007). Teaching students to shape the game: Negotiation architecture and the design of manageably dynamic simulations. *Negotiation Journal 23*(3), 333–342.

Weerawardena, J., & Sullivan Mort, G. (2006). Investigating social entrepreneurship: A multidimensional model. *Journal of World Business* 41 (2006), 21–35.

Welch, I. (2006). Ethics. Web chapter supplement to *Corporate Finance: An Introduction*, Boston: Addison-Wesley http://papers.ssrn.com/sol3/papers.cfm?abstract_id=876124

Welsh, N. A. (2006). Perceptions of fairness. In A. K. Schneider & C. Honeyman (Eds.). *The negotiator's field book: The desk reference for the experienced negotiator* (chapter 19). Washington, D.C.: ABA Section of Dispute Resolution.

Werbach, A. (2009). *Strategy for sustainability: A business manifesto*. Boston, MA: Harvard Business Press.

Wheeler, M. (2000). *Teaching negotiation: Ideas and innovations*. Cambridge, MA: PON Books.

Wheeler, M. (2004, March). Fair enough? An ethical fitness quiz for negotiators. *Negotiation newsletter* (pp. 1–4). Boston, MA: Harvard Business School Publishing.

Wheeler, M. (2006). Is teaching negotiation too easy, too hard, or both? *Negotiation Journal 22*(2), 187–197.

Whetten, D. A., & Delbecq, A. L. (2000). (Ed.) Saraide's chairman Hatim Tyabji on creating and sustaining a values-based organizational culture. *Academy of Management Executive 14*(4), 32–40.

Wilhelm, I. (2006, April 6). Fraud investigations raise new questions for beleaguered red cross. *Chronicle of Philanthropy 46*.

Williams, G. R., Farmer L. C., & Manwaring M. (2008). New technology meets and old teaching challenge: Using digital video recordings, annotation software, and deliberate practice techniques to improve student negotiation skills. *Negotiation Journal 24*(1), 71–86.

Wood, R. E., & Bandura, A. (1989). Social cognitive theory of organizational management. *Academy of Management Review 14*(365).

Young, D. R. (2001). Organizational identity in nonprofit organizations: strategic and structural implications'. *Nonprofit Management and Leadership 12*(2), 139–157.

Youngdahl, W. E. (2011). The space shuttle *Challenger* teleconference. Boston, MA: Harvard Business School Publishing (Product #TB0289-PDF-ENG).

Zack, G. M. (2003). *Fraud and abuse in nonprofit organisations: A guide to prevention and detection.* Hoboken, NJ: Wiley 2003.

Zadek, S. (2004). The path to corporate responsibility. *Harvard Business Review 82*(12), 125–132.

Zahra, S. A., Gedajlovic, E., Neubaum, D. O., & Shulman, J. M. (2009). A typology of social entrepreneurs: motives, search processes and ethical challenges. *Journal of Business Venturing 24*, 519–532.

Index

OTHER TITLES IN THE PRINCIPLES OF RESPONSIBLE MANAGEMENT EDUCATION (PRME) COLLECTION

Oliver Laasch, Monterrey Institute of Technology, Collection Editor

- *Business Integrity in Practice: Insights from International Case Studies* by Agata Stachowicz-Stanusch and Wolfgang Amann
- *Academic Ethos Management: Building the Foundation for Integrity in Management Education* by Agata Stachowicz-Stanusch
- *Responsible Management: Understanding Human Nature, Ethics, and Sustainability* by Kemi Ogunyemi
- *Fostering Spirituality in the Workplace: A Leader's Guide to Sustainability* by Priscilla Berry

FORTHCOMING TITLES ALSO IN THIS COLLECTION

- *Teaching Anticorruption: Developing a Foundation for Business Integrity* by Agata Stachowicz-Stanusch and Hans Krause Hansen
- *A Practical Guide to Educating for Responsibility in Management and Business* by Ross McDonald
- *Marketing to the Low-Income Consumer* by Paulo Cesar Motta
- *Managing Corporate Responsibility in Emerging Markets: Issues, Cases, and Solutions* by Jenik Radon and Mahima Achuthan

Announcing the Business Expert Press Digital Library

*Concise E-books Business Students Need
for Classroom and Research*

This book can also be purchased in an e-book collection by your library as
- a one-time purchase,
- that is owned forever,
- allows for simultaneous readers,
- has no restrictions on printing, and
- can be downloaded as PDFs from within the library community.

Our digital library collections are a great solution to beat the rising cost of textbooks. e-books can be loaded into their course management systems or onto student's e-book readers.

The **Business Expert Press** digital libraries are very affordable, with no obligation to buy in future years. For more information, please visit **www.businessexpertpress.com/librarians**. To set up a trial in the United States, please contact **Adam Chesler** at *adam.chesler@ businessexpertpress.com* for all other regions, contact **Nicole Lee** at *nicole.lee@igroupnet.com*.